# growing orchard fruits

# growing orchard fruits

a directory of varieties and how to
cultivate them successfully

**Richard Bird**
and **Kate Whiteman**

LORENZ BOOKS

This edition is published by Lorenz Books,
an imprint of Anness Publishing Ltd,
108 Great Russell Street,
London WC1B 3NA;
info@anness.com

www.lorenzbooks.com;
www.annesspublishing.com;
twitter: @Anness_Books

If you like the images in this book and would like to investigate using them for publishing, promotions or advertising, please visit our website www.practicalpictures.com for more information.

© Anness Publishing Ltd 2015

All rights reserved. No part of this publication may be reproduced, stored in a retrieval system, or transmitted in any way or by any means, electronic, mechanical, photocopying, recording or otherwise, without the prior written permission of the copyright holder.

A CIP catalogue record for this book is available from the British Library.

Publisher: Joanna Lorenz
Senior Editor: Felicity Forster
Photographers: Peter Anderson,
    Jonathan Buckley and Don Last
Jacket Photographer: Martin Brigdale
Designer: Paul Calver
Production Controller: Rosanna Anness

PUBLISHER'S NOTE
Although the advice and information in this book are believed to be accurate and true at the time of going to press, neither the authors nor the publisher can accept any legal responsibility or liability for any errors or omissions that may have been made nor for any inaccuracies nor for any loss, harm or injury that comes about from following instructions or advice in this book.

# Contents

| | |
|---|---|
| Introduction | 6 |
| **TYPES OF TREE FRUIT** | **8** |
| Apples | 10 |
| Pears | 12 |
| Cherries | 14 |
| Plums and damsons | 16 |
| Peaches and nectarines | 18 |
| Apricots | 20 |
| Citrus fruits | 21 |
| **PLANNING AND PREPARATION** | **24** |
| Types of soil | 26 |
| Improving the soil | 28 |
| Compost | 30 |
| Choosing fruit trees | 32 |
| Planting fruit trees | 34 |
| Supporting fruit trees | 36 |
| Pruning | 38 |
| Protecting fruit | 40 |
| Harvesting and storing | 42 |
| Pests and diseases | 44 |
| Growing tree fruit organically | 46 |
| Tools and equipment | 48 |
| **CULTIVATING TREE FRUIT** | **50** |
| Growing apples | 52 |
| Growing pears | 54 |
| Growing cherries | 56 |
| Growing plums and damsons | 58 |
| Growing peaches and nectarines | 60 |
| Growing apricots | 61 |
| Growing citrus fruits | 62 |
| Index | 64 |

# Introduction

The reasons for growing fruit in our gardens have never been more compelling. Fruits offer such a variety of colours, textures, scents and flavours, and they are good for us too – we should eat at least five portions of fruit and vegetables every day. Growing them yourself is much better than buying, as you can avoid the insecticides, fungicides and appearance-enhancers found on shop-bought produce.

It is widely recognized that fresh produce tastes better than fruit that has been sitting in an in-store display for days on end after having been transported, as often happens, half-way across the world. How much better, from the point of view of our health, and how much more rewarding, financially and from the point of view of our tastebuds and the environment, to grow at least one of the trees that produces a favourite fruit.

## GROWING ORCHARD FRUITS

In the past, when gardens were larger than they are today, it was not unusual for there to be at least two apple trees, one bearing dessert fruit, one bearing fruit for cooking, as well as a plum tree or two and, perhaps, a peach tree trained against a warm, sunny wall. Few gardens now have the space for more than one or, at the most, two free-standing standard trees, and many gardeners are deterred from growing fruit-bearing trees because they think they will involve too much work.

Nothing could be further from the truth. Indeed, when space is limited, the arguments in favour of including a fruit tree in a planting scheme become even stronger. Not only will the tree produce its summer or autumn crop, but it will also bear beautiful blossom in spring, and provide shade in summer and structure all year round, even when the leaves have fallen and the branches are bare. The development of dwarfing rootstocks means that even a standard fruit tree need not take up much space, while training techniques, such as espalier and cordon, mean that plants will take up the same amount of space as a hedge and can, in fact, often fulfil the same purpose. The annual pruning of fruit trees is actually no more onerous than the attention required by such gardeners' favourites as roses and clematis.

LEFT Growing a fruit tree against a wall or fence is a good method if you have limited space. The initial training demands patience and skill, but the tree will produce a good crop.

## HARVESTING TREE FRUIT

There could be few things simpler than plucking a ripe apple or pear from a tree to eat. When there are sufficient fruits to provide supplies for late autumn and winter, it will be necessary to provide a cool but frost-free space for storage. Late apples and pears finish ripening several weeks after they have been picked, and they should not, therefore, be stored with mid-season fruit until they are completely ripe, because the ripe fruit gives off gases that adversely affect the life of the still-ripening fruit. In addition, apples and pears should always be stored separately. Apples and pears can be frozen only if they are to be used in cooked dishes after thawing.

Fresh plums and damsons do not store well and are best picked when ripe for immediate use. Cherries, too, are best harvested and eaten as soon as they are ripe. They do not keep well fresh, although they can be frozen. Peaches, nectarines and apricots should be left to ripen on the branch before harvesting. Once picked, they should be eaten immediately or preserved in syrup. Apricots dry very well.

Unlike other tree fruits, oranges and lemons do not ripen at the same time, and individual fruits should be picked as they are ready or left on the tree until they are needed.

## COOKING WITH TREE FRUIT

Like most fruit, tree fruits are best enjoyed fresh from the garden, but they can be used in a wide range of dishes, although culinary varieties of apples, pears and plums usually survive the cooking process better than dessert varieties. If you have room for only one type of tree fruit, look for dual-purpose varieties. The pears 'Red Comice' and 'Pitmaston Duchess' are good for both cooking and eating, for example, as is the plum 'Early Laxton'. Sour cherries are usually grown for cooking in pies and jams, and although sweet cherries are generally regarded as a dessert fruit they can be cooked in similar recipes. In the same way, dessert varieties of plums, greengages and damsons can be used in pies and jams, although culinary varieties of the same fruits are usually too acid and tart to be eaten raw. Those citrus fruits that are not eaten fresh are traditionally made into marmalade.

ABOVE Freshly harvested tree fruits, ready for eating raw or to be used in cooking.

BELOW The zesty flavour of lemons can be enjoyed to the utmost in a fresh tart.

# types of tree fruit

The expression "tree fruits" is used to distinguish these fruits from cane and soft fruit, such as berries and currants. It describes some of the most widely grown and widely eaten fruit – cooking and dessert apples and pears – as well as some of the most popular of summer fruits – peaches, nectarines and apricots. Although they do not immediately spring to mind as garden plants, citrus trees can be grown successfully in containers as long as they can be protected from the worst of the winter weather.

# Apples

Grown in many countries around the world, apples are a staple fruit, but although there are thousands of varieties, the number available in shops can be limited. Unlike many fruits, of which the taste differs only marginally from one type to another, apples exhibit a great range of flavours and textures. In addition, some are suitable for cooking, others are dessert (eating) apples, and others combine both qualities.

Many even quite large garden centres carry only a limited range, and you will find a better selection if you can visit one of the open days held by specialist apple nurseries. It is usually possible to taste several different varieties of ripe fruit and see the trees themselves, which you can often buy or order.

### HISTORY

Apples have been eaten since prehistoric times, when only wild crab apples existed. The Romans adored apples and were the first people to cultivate the fruit; by the 1st century AD they were growing at least a dozen varieties throughout the Roman Empire.

'Egremont Russet'

### VARIETIES

With over 7,000 named varieties of apples, it would be impossible to list more than a tiny fraction. The advantage of growing apples yourself is that nurseries can supply many more varieties than the dozen types you find in most shops, and they will taste better too.

'Braeburn' is a crisp, juicy apple with a smooth, pale green skin, heavily flushed with red, and makes excellent eating. 'Braeburn' apples are grown mainly in the southern hemisphere, as they need plenty of daylight.

### VARIETIES

**Dessert (eating)**
'Blenheim Orange'
'Braeburn'
'Cox's Orange Pippin'
'Discovery'
'Egremont Russet'
'Gala'
'Golden Delicious'
'Granny Smith'
'Idared'
'James Grieve'
'Laxton's Superb'
'Lord Lambourne'
'Ribston Pippin'
'Sturmer Pippin'
'Worcester Pearmain'

**Cooking**
'Bramley's Seedling'
'Grenadier'
'Howgate Wonder'
'Lord Derby'
'Newton Wonder'

'Bramley's Seedling'

'Bramley's Seedling' is a large, flattish, red-flushed green cooking apple. It has coarse, white, juicy, acid flesh that cooks into a purée.

'Egremont Russet' is the most readily available of a number of russet apples, all of which have rough, porous skins that allow the water to evaporate, giving a denser flesh and intensifying the nutty flavour.

'Gala' is a colourful eating apple from New Zealand with a yellow ground colour flushed with bright orange and red. 'Royal Gala' is similar, but red all over.

'Golden Delicious', a conical, freckled, golden apple originally grown from a chance seedling in the USA, has become ubiquitous.

'Granny Smith' was first grown in Australia in the early 1860s from a seedling noticed by Mrs Thomas Smith. This largish, all-purpose, rather tart apple is bright green, turning yellow as it ripens.

'Worcester Pearmain' is a conical, green apple flushed with bright red. The juicy white flesh has a hint of strawberry flavour. They are best eaten straight from the tree.

## NUTRITION

Apples were once believed to be the most nutritious of fruits, giving rise to the saying that "an apple a day keeps the doctor away". In fact, they have fewer vitamins than many other fruits (although they contain some vitamins C and A), but they are high in pectin and are a good source of dietary fibre. They provide 52 kilocalories per 100g/3¾oz.

## STORING

Apples should not be washed before storing, but only when ready to use. Store at the bottom of the refrigerator in the salad crisper.

'Worcester Pearmain'

### MAKING APPLE SAUCE

Peel, core and thickly slice the apples, immediately dropping the pieces into a bowl of cold water acidulated with lemon juice or cider vinegar.

Barely cover the bottom of a pan with cold water. Add the apple pieces and cook to a purée, adding butter and sugar to taste towards the end.

If you are using firmer dessert apples, cook until very tender, then rub through a coarse sieve.

'Golden Delicious'

TYPES OF TREE FRUIT  11

# Pears

There are almost as many varieties of pears as there are apples, but fewer than a dozen are available in the shops. Pears are similar to apples, but are more fragile and are more often eaten raw than cooked. They have fine white, granular flesh and a central core containing the pips. Most pears have the familiar shape, wider at the bottom than the top, but some are shaped like apples, while "calabash" pears have an elongated neck, like a gourd. Pears are less vividly coloured than apples, generally varying from bronze to gold, green or yellow, but there are some beautiful red varieties available.

'Anjou'

## HISTORY

Wild pears are native to Europe and Asia, where they have grown since prehistoric times. They were cultivated by the ancient Phoenicians and the Romans, and they became a royal delicacy for the ancient Persian kings. Their popularity spread so fast that in medieval Italy more than 200 varieties of pear were cultivated. By the early 18th century the French were growing 300 different varieties, inspired by Louis XIV's passion for the fruit. There are now said to be more than 5,000 named varieties throughout the world.

## VARIETIES

Cooking pears do exist, but almost all pears available are dessert fruit, which can also be cooked. Pears are seasonal, so only a few varieties are available at any one time. 'Anjou' are large pears, also known as 'Beurre d'Anjou', with greenish-yellow skin with brown speckles or russeting. The flesh is sweet. They are suitable for eating and cooking.

'Conference'

### VARIETIES

'Anjou'
'Beth'
'Beurré Hardy'
'Black Worcester'
'Concorde'
'Conference'
'Doyenné du Comice'
'Durondeau'
'Forelle'
'Glou Morceau'
'Jargonelle'
'Joséphine de Malines'
'Louise Bonne of Jersey'
'Merton Pride'
'Onward'
'Packham's Triumph'
'Williams' Bon Chrétien'

'Conference', first cultivated in Berkshire in 1770, have remained a favourite in Britain, largely because they keep so well. They are long, conical pears, yellowish-green with extensive russeting, and they turn yellower when they are mature. The granular flesh is tender, sweet and juicy. They are excellent for eating and cooking.

'Doyenné du Comice'

'Doyenné du Comice' is a large, roundish pear, one of the finest of all, with creamy white, melting, very juicy flesh and a sweet, aromatic flavour. The thick, yellowish-green skin is covered with speckles and patches of russetting. These pears are best eaten raw and are delicious with Brie or Camembert cheese.

'Forelle', which originated in Germany, is a rounded, conical dessert pear with a shiny skin covered with pinkish-red dots (hence the name: the word *Forelle* means "trout"). The well-flavoured flesh is very sweet and tender.

'Packham's Triumph' was the first successful Australian pear produced by Charles Packham in 1896, and still a favourite. A largish dessert pear, it has a smooth, green, lightly russetted skin, which changes to bright yellow as it ripens. The soft, white flesh is succulent and sweet, with just a touch of acidity.

'Williams' Bon Chrétien' are irregularly shaped pears, known as 'Bartlett' in the USA, generally swollen on one side of the stalk. The speckled skin is golden-yellow with russet patches and sometimes a red tinge. The delicious tender flesh is creamy-white and very juicy, and the flavour is sweet and slightly musky. They are suitable for cooking and eating.

'Forelle'

'Packham's Triumph'

'Williams' Bon Chrétien'

### NUTRITION
Pears contain small amounts of vitamins A and C and some potassium and riboflavin. They provide about 60 kilocalories per 100g/3¾oz.

### STORING
Test a pear for ripeness by pressing the stem end between your forefinger and thumb; it should give a little, but the pear should still be quite firm. Once ripe, pears should be eaten within a couple of days, or they will quickly become woolly or squashy and unpleasant.

Ripe pears should be stored at the bottom of the refrigerator in the salad crisper. Do not refrigerate unripe fruit – they will not ripen in the cold. Keep unripe fruit in a bowl at room temperature or in a cool, dark place until ready to eat.

### PREVENTING DISCOLORATION

Pears quickly turn brown when exposed to the air. To prevent discoloration, brush cut pears with lemon juice or acidulate a bowl of cold water with lemon juice. Drop the cut pears into the bowl immediately after preparing.

# Cherries

'Colney'

Blossoming cherry trees are one of the great delights of spring, followed in summer by clusters of bright shiny fruit hanging in pairs from long, elegant stalks. The skin of these small, round stone fruits can vary in colour from pale creamy-yellow to deepest red or almost black. The firm, juicy flesh can be sweet or sour, depending on the variety, of which there are hundreds. Cherries are categorized into three main groups: sweet (for eating), sour (for cooking) and hybrids, such as the nobly named Dukes or Royals, which are suitable for eating raw or cooking.

## HISTORY

The original wild sweet cherries, known as mazzards, were found in Asia Minor and were cultivated by the Chinese 3,000 years ago. Mazzards were known to the Ancient Egyptians, Greeks and Romans, and still exist today. Sour (or acid) cherries were brought to Rome from Greece, and all modern varieties derive from these early specimens.

## VARIETIES

Sweet cherries are derived from *Prunus avium*, and they used to be divided into two main groups, bigarreaus and geans (or guignes). Now, however, they are usually classified by fruiting time: early, mid-season or late. Sour cherries, which are derived from *P. cerasus*, are of two main types, the dark-fruited 'Morello' cherries and the light to mid-red 'Amarelle' cherries. Most sour cherries are too tart to eat raw, but they are ideal for cooking and are also used in the manufacture of liqueurs. Duke or Royal cherries (*P. × gondouinii*) are believed to be a cross between sweet and sour cherries. The fruits, which may be either black or red, are good for cooking, and the trees are hardy.

Maraschino cherries (*P. cerasus* var. *marasca*), a sort of bitter, dark red cherry native to Dalmatia, are distilled to produce a cordial or liqueur. The bright red, bottled maraschino cherries, which are used to decorate cocktails and cakes, tend to be ordinary cherries, tinted with artificial colour and steeped in almond-flavoured syrup.

### Sweet Cherries

'Bigarreau Napoleon' has large, rather heart-shaped fruits, red or red-flushed yellow, which are borne late in the season. This is not a

> ### VARIETIES
>
> **Sweet**
> 'Bigarreau Napoleon'
> 'Bing'
> 'Colney'
> 'Early Rivers'
> 'Governor Wood'
> 'Greenstem Black'
> 'Kent Bigarreau'
> 'Lapins'
> 'Merton Bigarreau'
> 'Merton Favourite'
> 'Merton Glory'
> 'Noir de Guben'
> 'Stella'
> 'Waterloo'
>
> **Sour or acid**
> 'Kentish Red'
> 'May Duke'
> 'Montmorency'
> 'Morello'
> 'Nabella'
> 'Reine Hortense'
> 'The Flemish'

'Bigarreau Napoleon'

'Bing'

## Sour Cherries

'Kentish Red' is an Amarelle type with smallish, scarlet fruit. The soft, juicy, yellow flesh has a bitter, rather acid flavour. The plants have good resistance to canker.

### PITTING CHERRIES

Special gadgets make this fiddly task easy. Put the fruit in a cherry pitter and push the bar into the fruit. The pit will be ejected.

self-fertile cherry and the trees are susceptible to canker disease when grown in poorly drained, heavy soil.

'Bing' is a US mid-season cherry, developed in Oregon, which has dark, mahogany-red, juicy fruits. Sadly, it is not self-fertile, but the cultivar 'Garden Bing' is self-fertile and will do well in a container.

'Colney' is a late season dessert variety with very dark red skins and a sweet, juicy taste.

'Early Rivers' has large, round, black fruits with red flesh and juice. This is one of the earliest cherries to flower and to bear fruit, and it is a reliable and heavy cropper.

'Lapins' is a self-fertile plant from Canada, sometimes sold as 'Cherokee', which produces a good crop of firm-textured, juicy, dark red fruits late in the season.

'Stella', originating from British Columbia, is a late cherry producing good crops of large, dark red fruits. It has the additional advantages that it is resistant to canker and is self-fertile.

'Morello' is the best known and most widely planted of the sour cherries, and its name has become synonymous with the type. The fruits are bright, glossy red and the soft, juicy flesh is sharp but not over-acidic. It is a reliable and heavy cropper, and the plants are self-fertile.

'Nabella' is a heavy-cropping cherry which originated in Germany. It is a self-fertile form, producing very dark red fruits.

## NUTRITION

Cherries contain vitamins A and C and some dietary fibre. They are a good source of potassium. Their calorie content varies with the type; sweet cherries provide about 77 kilocalories per 100g/3¾oz, while the same quantity of sour fruit provides about 56 kilocalories.

## STORING

Unwashed cherries will keep for a few days in the refrigerator; wash them just before serving. They can also be removed from their stems and frozen.

'Morello'

### TYPES OF TREE FRUIT 15

# Plums and damsons

There are thousands of varieties of plum, all differing in size, shape, colour and flavour. These members of the rose family originate from three main types: European, Japanese and Western Asian. The skins can vary from blue-black to purple, red, green and yellow. They have a long season, and one variety or another is available almost all year round. All plums have smooth skins with a bloom and juicy flesh with plenty of acidity.

Dessert plums can be eaten on their own; they are usually larger than cooking plums (up to 10cm/ 4in long) and are sweet and very juicy. Cooking plums are drier, with tart flesh.

'Angelino'

## HISTORY
Wild plums originated in Asia at least 2,000 years ago. They were first cultivated by the Assyrians, then adopted by the Romans, who hybridized them with great enthusiasm; the historian Pliny wrote of the huge numbers of plum cross-breeds available. The Crusaders brought plums to Europe, where they became highly prized. Nowadays they are grown in almost all temperate countries.

## VARIETIES
There are more than 2,000 varieties of plum, all derived from *Prunus domestica*, but only a few are regularly offered for sale. Both dessert and cooking plums are usually classified by fruiting time – early, mid-season and late – so if you have space in your garden, it is possible to have fruit over a long period.

Closely related to plums are damsons and mirabelles (*Prunus insititia*). Damsons, small, plum-like fruits, have deep blue-black skins with an attractive bloom. The flavour is strong and tart, which makes them more suitable for cooking than for eating raw; they freeze well. They grow wild in hedgerows but are also commercially available. Mirabelles, sometimes known as cherry plums, are round and grow on long stalks, like cherries. They have black, red or yellow skins, which can taste rather bitter, but all have sweet, juicy flesh.

### VARIETIES
**Dessert**
'Angelino'
'Bradley's King'
'Cambridge Gage'
'Coe's Golden Drop'
'Early Laxton'
'Green Gage Group'
'Jefferson'
'Kirke's'
'Merton Gem'
'Oullins Gage'
'Victoria'

**Cooking**
'Czar'
'Early Rivers'
'Laxton's Cropper'
'Marjorie's Seedling'
'Mirabelle'
'Pershore'
'Reeves'

'Marjorie's Seedling'

'Reeves'

Golden mirabelles are delicious in tarts and soufflés, and are also made into a colourless brandy.

'Angelino' is a large, meaty plum with purple skin and tasty, yellow flesh. It is good for making jams and tarts.

'Bradley's King' is a prolific damson, bearing sweet, almost black fruits.

'Czar' has early fruits with dark purple skin and juicy, yellowish-green flesh. It is an excellent, heavy-cropping culinary plum.

'Marjorie's Seedling' bears large, late, purple plums with a green flush. They have bitter skins and sweet, green, almost translucent flesh. Although usually sold as a culinary plum, the ripe fruit is delicious raw.

'Mirabelle' has well-flavoured, small, golden-yellow fruits with rather dry, yellow flesh.

'Oullins Gage' bears large, round fruits with green-dotted, yellow skin and pale yellow, almost translucent flesh. The fruit is good for eating raw and for freezing.

'Reeves' is a heavy cropping cooking variety of Canadian origin, with red skin.

'Victoria', perhaps the best known of all dessert plums, was first cultivated in 1840 from a stray seedling found in Sussex, England.

'Victoria'

The large, sweet, juicy fruits have scarlet-flushed, yellow skins when ripe. They are good raw and for bottling, canning and stewing.

damsons

### PREPARING AND COOKING PLUMS

Dessert plums are delicious eaten on their own. Dual varieties (suitable for eating and cooking) and cooking plums make excellent pies and tarts, compotes, crumbles, dumplings, sauces, mousses and soufflés. They can be poached, baked or stewed, either whole or in halves or slices. It is not recommended that plums with tough skins are cooked in the microwave, as they will not soften in the short cooking time. Cook plums until just tender; do not let them disintegrate.

### NUTRITION

Plums contain more antioxidant than any other fruit. They also contain about 10 per cent sugar, of which half is glucose. They provide about 40 kilocalories per 100g/3¾oz.

### STORING

Plums ripen fast, and quickly become overripe, so store them in the refrigerator for only a day or two. For cooking at a later date, plums can be frozen. Halve the fruit and remove the pits first.

# Peaches and nectarines

These two fruits originated from the same species. They are very similar, except that peaches have fuzzy skin, while nectarines are smooth. So alike are they, in fact, that peach trees sometimes spontaneously produce nectarines and vice versa. Nectarines are sometimes crossed with peaches, but the fuzzy peach skin tends to be dominant, and the resulting hybrids are often actually peaches.

Sometimes known as the queen of fruits, peaches (*Prunus persica*) are certainly among the most beautiful. The downy, velvety skin is yellow, flushed with red, and they are voluptuously curved; the French call one variety 'Les Tétons de Vénus' ("the breasts of Venus").

The most familiar peaches are round or "beaked" – that is, they have a slightly pointed end – but they can also be rather flat and disc-shaped. The delicate, fine-textured flesh, which can be yellow, white or flushed with red, encloses a heavily ridged stone or pit. In some peaches the flesh clings to the stone; these are known as clingstone or cling peaches, and they usually have firm flesh. In others, known as freestone peaches, the flesh comes away cleanly and easily from the stone; these have soft flesh. Peaches are, in fact, usually sold by the colour of their flesh – yellow or white – and some people believe that those with white flesh have the superior flavour.

The flavour of nectarines (*P. persica* var. *nectarina*) is very similar to that of peaches, although it is slightly more acidic. The flesh can be yellow, white or pinkish and is delicate and sweet. Some people, who dislike eating the skin of peaches, prefer nectarines as a dessert fruit. They can be cooked in the same ways as peaches.

## HISTORY

Peaches are native to mountainous areas of Korea, Tibet and western China, and they have been cultivated in China since at least the 5th century BC. They are regarded as symbols of longevity, and even today some Chinese families place peach trees outside their front doors to ward off evil spirits. The Greeks and Romans found peaches growing in Persia and, believing that they originated there, gave them the name "persica". The fruits or seeds reached Asia Minor via the old silk route from China and were planted in the countries of the eastern Mediterranean.

Widely grown throughout Europe, peaches and nectarines were introduced to America by Christopher Columbus in the 15th century, and they became so profuse that it was once believed that they were indigenous to North America. Now, so many are grown in Georgia that it is known as the peach state.

## VARIETIES

Although peaches and nectarines are seldom sold by variety in shops, many reliable named forms are available to grow.

'Bellegarde' is a late-cropping peach with warm, yellow skin, almost covered with deep red

> **VARIETIES**
>
> **Peaches**
> 'Amsden June'
> 'Bellegarde'
> 'Duke of York'
> 'Dymond'
> 'Garden Lady'
> 'Peregrine'
> 'Redhaven'
> 'Rochester'
> 'Royal George'
>
> **Nectarines**
> 'Independence'
> 'John Rivers'
> 'Lord Napier'
> 'Pineapple'

'Peregrine'

'Garden Lady'

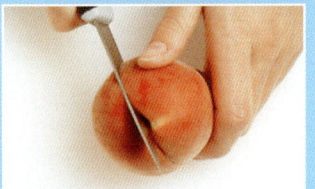

## PITTING A PEACH OR NECTARINE

Slice through the seam line all around the peach.

Twist the two halves in opposite directions to separate them.

The pit can be levered out with a knife.

mottling. The flavourful flesh is firm and white. This is an old French variety, best grown against a warm wall or under glass.

'Garden Lady', a naturally dwarf form, is a mid-season peach from New Zealand with yellow fruit flushed with bright red, with juicy, sweet, yellow flesh. This is an ideal peach for a container.

'Lord Napier' is a heavy, mid-season cropper, one of the most widely grown nectarines. It has large, yellow-orange fruits, flushed with red, with white flesh.

'Peregrine' is an old variety of peach for mid-season cropping. Its skin is blushed deep red and its contrasting greenish-white flesh has a juicy flavour.

'Pineapple' is considered by many to be one of the best flavoured nectarines. The taste is reminiscent of pineapple. It is a late season variety. The skin is yellow, streaked with crimson, and the flesh is yellow.

'Royal George' is a late season peach with an exceptionally fine flavour. The skin is blushed and speckled in red and the flesh is yellow. The fruits are large and juicy. This is one of the oldest British varieties of peach.

### NUTRITION

Peaches are a source of vitamins A, B and C and provide about 60 kilocalories per 100g/3¾oz. Nectarines have a lower calorie count than peaches, containing only about 45 kilocalories per 100g/3¾oz. They are a good source of potassium and phosphorus, dietary fibre and vitamins A and C.

nectarines

### STORING

Peaches and nectarines do not ripen successfully after picking. The fruits should be handled carefully. Press gently to ensure that they are firm, with some "give". Never pick greenish fruit, except for chutney-making, and avoid fruit with bruised skin. Firm fruit can be kept at room temperature for a day or two to soften; ripe fruit can be kept in the fridge for not more than two days.

# Apricots

These round, yellow-orange fruits have velvety skins flushed with pink. The flesh is firm, sweet and fragrant and contains little juice. The kernel of the stone is edible and is used to flavour jams, biscuits (cookies) and amaretto liqueur.

## HISTORY

Apricots grew wild in China thousands of years ago and were introduced to Persia and Armenia, from where they got their Latin name, *Prunus armeniaca*. Alexander the Great brought apricots to southern Europe, where they were prized by the Romans and Greeks, who called them "golden eggs of the sun". They were first successfully cultivated in northern Europe in the 16th century.

## VARIETIES

Like plums, different varieties of apricots are usually classified according to their fruiting time – early, mid-season or late.

'Moorpark' is a popular mid- to late season variety. It produces large, excellent-flavoured fruit with pale yellow skins flushed with red and orange-coloured flesh.

'Hemskirke' is an early, hardy variety with large yellow fruit with red blotches and an orange flesh.

'Luizet' is an old French variety producing large fruits that have a yellow-orange skin, blushed with carmine red. The perfumed flesh is yellow-orange, sweet and reasonably juicy. It can be grown as a standard tree.

'Polonais' is another French variety. It is an early variety with a pale yellow-orange skin and orange-yellow flesh. It is sweetly flavoured with a delightful smell. It is useful for preserving.

dried apricots

### VARIETIES

'Alfred'
'Bergeron'
'Breda'
'Early Moorpark'
'Hemskirke'
'Luizet'
'Moorpark'
'New Large Early'
'Polonais'

## NUTRITION

Apricots contain the antioxidant beta-carotene, and are a rich source of minerals and vitamin A. They provide only about 30 kilocalories per 100g/3¾oz.

## STORING

Apricots do not travel well, nor do they continue to ripen after picking, so pick plump fruit with a rich colour and smooth skin. Keep apricots at room temperature for a couple of days or store them in the fridge for up to five days. They can be preserved by drying.

### SAUTÉEING APRICOTS

Slice or dice the fruit (peel it or not, as you wish) and toss quickly in hot butter until lightly browned all over. Add sugar and flavourings to taste.

fresh apricots

# Citrus fruits

No family of fruits seems to store up sunshine more successfully than citrus fruits. All citrus fruits have tough, bitter peel that is highly scented and contains aromatic essential oils. Inside, the fruit is segmented and encloses juicy flesh, with a more or less acid flavour, around the seeds. The fruits ripen on the tree and do not continue to develop after picking, so they have excellent keeping qualities.

lemons

## GRAPEFRUITS

One of the largest citrus fruits, grapefruits can vary in diameter from 10cm/4in to 18cm/7in. Most have deep yellow skins, but the flesh can range from very pale yellow (confusingly called "white"), through rosy pink to deep pink (known as "ruby"). In general, the pinker the flesh, the sweeter the grapefruit will be.

Very low in calories (only about 43 kilocalories per 100g/3¾oz), grapefruit are an excellent source of dietary fibre and vitamin C; one fruit provides one-and-a-half times the adult daily requirement of this vitamin.

## LEMONS

Arguably the most useful of all fruit, the distinctively shaped lemon can be very large or quite small, with thick or thin, smooth or knobbly skin. The skin contains aromatic essential oils, and a good lemon will perfume the air with its fragrance. The juicy, pale yellow, acid flesh enhances almost any other food and never fails to refresh the tastebuds. Rich in vitamin C and very low in calories, lemons only provide about 22 kilocalories per 100g/3¾oz.

grapefruits

### VARIETIES

**Grapefruits**
'Foster'
'Navel'
'Star Ruby'

**Lemons**
'Fino'
'Garey's Eureka'
'Lisbon'
'Toscana'

**Limes**
'Indian'
'Persian'

**Kumquats**
*Fortunella japonica*
*Fortunella margarita*

**Tangerines**
'Clementine'
'Mandarin'
'Satsuma'

**Oranges**
'Lane Late'
'Malta Blood'
'Navelina'
'Seville'
'Valencia Late'
'Washington'

### ZESTING A LEMON

Holding an unwaxed lemon firmly in one hand, scrape a zester down the length of the lemon to pare off fine slivers of zest but not the white skin.

TYPES OF TREE FRUIT

## LIMES

The smallest members of the true citrus family, limes are about 5–6cm/2–2½in long. They are smaller, rounder and more squat than lemons, and have thin, fairly smooth, green skins and a highly aromatic, acid flavour. They grow in tropical regions and are an essential ingredient of South-east Asian, Mexican, Latin American and Caribbean cooking.

limes

'Indian' is a small, oval lime with a strong, sharp flavour.

'Persian' is a large lime with fine pulp and an acidic flavour.

Limes are high in vitamin C, contain some potassium, calcium and phosphorus, and provide about 20 kilocalories per 100g/3¾oz.

## KUMQUATS

Not true citrus fruits, kumquats belong to a similar genus, *Fortunella*. Their name comes from the Cantonese *kam kwat*, meaning "golden orange". The small, elongated fruits are about the size and shape of a large olive, with thin orange rind. The rind is sweeter than the sour pulp, and the two parts eaten together provide a delicious sour-sweet sensation. They are used in chutneys and jellies.

Kumquats are a source of vitamins C and A and have some calcium, phosphorus and riboflavin. They provide about 65 kilocalories per 100g/3¾oz.

## TANGERINES

Sometimes known as "easy peelers", tangerines are part of a large family of small citrus fruit. They resemble slightly flattened oranges with loose orange skins and have a fragrant aroma, which is inextricably bound up with Christmas. All members of the tangerine family have aromatic skins, which can easily be detached from the segments (unlike oranges and lemons), and segments that separate easily. The flesh is sweet and perfumed, but often contains a large number of seeds.

The names of many types of tangerine are often interchanged, so you may find a bewildering variety of fruits that are essentially the same – for example, clementines, mandarins and satsumas.

'Clementine' is the smallest of the tangerines, with bright orange skin and no seeds.

ABOVE Easy to peel, satsumas have a refreshing tart flavour.

'Mandarin' has deliciously sweet segments, which make an attractive decoration for desserts.

'Satsuma' is a largish tangerine from Japan. It has loose skin and a refreshing, rather tart flavour.

All tangerines are extremely good sources of vitamin C and beta-carotene. They provide about 40 kilocalories per 100g/3¾oz.

## ORANGES

Despite their name, oranges are not always orange; they can also be yellow or mottled with red. The size can vary too – an orange can be as large as a football or as small as a cherry – and the flavour can range from sweet to intensely sour.

kumquats

'Valencia Late' oranges

## PEELING AND SEGMENTING ORANGES

Using a serrated knife, cut a thin slice from each end of the orange to expose the flesh.

Cut off the peel in a circular motion, removing the white pith as you go.

Hold the fruit over a bowl to catch the juice. Cut each segment between the membranes.

Squeeze out all the juice, making sure that all seeds are removed.

Oranges originated in China. They were probably known to the Ancient Greeks and may have been the mythical Golden Apples of the Hesperides. If so, they would have been bitter oranges, which were the only variety known at the time.

Over the centuries, traders took oranges to India, Arabia and then the Mediterranean. When the first oranges reached Europe, they were so rare that they became a symbol of opulence, to be offered as luxury gifts. The oranges were too precious to be eaten raw (in any case, they would have been too sour), but were made into preserves. The first sweet oranges to arrive in Europe were brought from India by traders in the 17th century. They became popular and were served as theatre refreshments.

Oranges fall into two groups: sweet oranges (*Citrus sinensis*), which can be eaten raw, and bitter oranges (*C. aurantium*), which cannot.

### Sweet Oranges

'Navelina' are seedless oranges, taking their name from the navel-like protuberance at the end, which contains a tiny embryonic fruit. They have thick, pebbly skins and very sweet, juicy flesh.

'Valencia Late' have smooth skins and contain few or no seeds. They are the world's most popular variety of orange.

### Bitter Oranges

'Seville' or 'Bigarade' is the most common bitter orange – vast numbers are grown in Seville, Spain. They are used in the classic *sauce bigarade*, which is traditionally served with roast duck.

## STORING

Citrus fruits do not ripen once picked, and can be kept in a cool room for at least a week. Oranges and lemons store well and can be kept for up to two weeks; limes and tangerines keep for one week.

# planning and preparation

Tree fruits differ from most other types of fruit grown in the garden in that the plants are permanent features, remaining in the same position for many years and even often outliving the person who planted them. Preparing the ground before planting is, therefore, one of the most important activities in the fruit garden. In addition, because these plants are often trained as espaliers or cordons, it is necessary to erect sturdy frames and wires against which they can be supported.

# Types of soil

With the exception of citrus fruits, which need acid soil, fruit trees can be grown on almost any type of soil, but rich, fertile, well-drained loam is the optimum, with a pH range of 6.5–7. Most soils can be persuaded to move towards the optimum, but soils vary in different areas and some are easier to deal with than others.

## CLAY SOILS

These can be fertile, but their structure is the despair of most gardeners. Clay is heavy, and the particles cling together, making the soil sticky. It compacts easily, forming a solid lump that roots find hard to penetrate and that is difficult to dig. Walking on the soil when wet will exacerbate this problem. This tendency to become compacted and sticky means that clay soils are slow to drain but, once dry, they "set" like concrete. They also tend to be cold and slow to warm up, making plants slow to start into growth.

Despite the difficulties of gardening on clay, you can achieve good results with most fruit trees, if you add plenty of organic matter and perhaps some grit, too, to improve drainage. Clay soils are usually rich, and all the hard effort needed in the initial stages to improve the soil will pay off in the long term.

## SANDY SOILS

Soils that are made up of sand and silts are quite different. They have few of the sticky clay particles but are made up of larger grains, which allow the water to pass through quickly. This quick passage of water through the soil tends to leach (wash) out nutrients, so the soils are often poor. But they also tend to be much warmer in winter and are quicker to warm in spring, so that plants begin to grow early in the year. Silts contain particles that are a bit more clay-like in texture than those found in sandy soils, and they hold more moisture and nutrients.

### pH VALUES

| | |
|---|---|
| 1.0 | extremely acid |
| 4.0 | maximum acidity tolerated by most plants |
| 5.5 | maximum acidity for reasonable vegetables |
| 6.0 | maximum acidity for most fruit and vegetables |
| 6.5 | optimum for the best fruit and vegetables |
| 7.0 | neutral, maximum alkalinity for good fruit and vegetables |
| 7.5 | maximum alkalinity for reasonable vegetables |
| 8.0 | maximum tolerated by most plants |
| 14.0 | extremely alkaline |

Both types of soil are easy to improve and are not difficult to work. Sand does not compact like clay does (although it is still not good practice to walk on cultivated ground), but silty soils are more susceptible to the continual impact of feet and wheelbarrows. Adding organic material can temper their insatiable thirst.

## LOAMS

The soil of most gardeners' dreams is loam. This is a combination of clay and sandy soils, with the best elements of both. They tend to be free draining, yet moisture retentive. This description – free draining and moisture retentive – is often used of soils and potting mixes, and it may seem a contradiction. It means that the soil allows excess moisture to

### WORKING IN ORGANIC MATTER

**1** Soil that has been dug in the autumn can have more organic matter worked into the top layer in the spring. Spread the organic matter over the surface.

**2** Lightly work the organic material into the top layer of soil with a fork. There is no need for full-scale digging because worms will take the humus down.

drain away so that some air is available to the plants' roots, but enough moisture is retained for the plants to take up what they need. Such soils are easy to work at any time, and they warm up well in spring, thus allowing plants to start into growth early in the year.

## ACID AND ALKALINE SOILS

Another way of classifying soils is by their acidity or alkalinity. Those that are based on peat (peat moss) are acid; those that include chalk or limestone are alkaline. Gardeners use a scale of pH levels to indicate the degree of acidity or alkalinity. Very acid is 1, neutral is 7 and very alkaline is 14, although soils rarely have values at the extremes of the scale. Although they can be grown on a wider range of soils, fruit trees are usually grown in soils with a pH of 5.5–7.5, with the optimum conditions being around 6.5, or slightly on the acid side of neutral. A test with a soil kit will show the rating in your own garden. Soil acidity can be reduced by adding lime, but it is not usually possible to convert an alkaline soil to a more acid one.

## IMPROVING HEAVY SOIL

In many gardens wet, poorly drained soil can be improved simply by adding organic material. The fibrous material contained in the organic matter helps to break up the clay particles, allowing water to pass through.

The other method is to add grit to the soil. The best material for this is grit up to about 5mm/¼in in diameter. Flint grit that has been crushed is best because the angular faces allow water to drain away better than the rounded surfaces of uncrushed grit, such as peabeach.

### TESTING THE SOIL FOR NUTRIENTS

1 Collect the soil sample 5–8cm/2–3in below the surface. Take a number of samples, but test each one separately.

2 With this kit, mix one part of soil with five parts of water. Shake well in a jar, then allow the water to settle.

3 Draw off some of the settled liquid from the top few centimetres (about an inch) for your test.

4 Carefully transfer the solution to the test chamber in the plastic container, using the pipette.

5 Select a colour-coded capsule (one for each nutrient). Put the powder in the chamber, replace the cap and shake.

6 After a few minutes, compare the colour of the liquid with the shade panel of the container.

PLANNING AND PREPARATION

# Improving the soil

Perhaps the most important task in any garden is to improve and maintain the quality of the soil. Achieving good-quality soil should be the aim of any gardener who wants to plant fruit trees. To ignore the soil is to ignore one of the garden's greatest assets.

## FRUIT PLANTINGS
For any type of plant that will be in position for several years, it is important that the soil is in the best possible condition before planting begins. After planting it will be impossible to dig in more material, and you will have to depend on top-dressing. Although this is a good supplement, it is not an alternative to proper preparation in the first place. The ground should be double dug if possible, and you should add as much organic matter as you can get, especially in the lower layers of soil.

## ORGANIC MATERIAL
Adding organic material will benefit all soil types: it helps to break up heavy clay, improving the drainage, while sandy soil will be made more moisture retentive. Most types of organic matter also add a good range of nutrients. Useful materials include rotted garden waste, kitchen vegetable waste, farmyard manures, leafmould and other plant waste material, such as grass clippings.

It is important that any such material should be well-rotted. If it is still in the process of breaking down, it will need nitrogen to complete the process and will extract it from the soil. This, of course, is the reverse of what the gardener wants – the gardener's aim is, in fact, to add nitrogen to the soil. If you are unsure, a good indicator that the material has broken down sufficiently is that it becomes odourless.

## DIGGING IN
The best way to introduce organic material into the garden is to dig it in. In this way it becomes incorporated into the soil. If possible, double dig the bed, adding material all the way to the bottom of both spits. This will help to retain moisture and supply nutrients where they are needed, which is down by the roots. It will also encourage roots to delve deeply rather than remaining on the surface. The deeper the roots go the more stable will be the plant's water supply and the plant will grow at a regular pace rather than in unproductive fits and starts.

## TOP-DRESSING
Once the ground has been planted, especially with permanent fruit trees, you will not be able to dig in organic matter without damaging the roots of the trees. However,

### IMPROVING SOIL STRUCTURE

**1** One of the best ways to improve the structure of the soil is to add as much organic material as you can, preferably when the soil is dug. For heavy soils, this is best done in the autumn.

**2** If the soil has already been dug, well-rotted organic material can be worked into the surface of the soil with a fork. The worms will complete the task of working it into the soil.

LEFT The fertility of the soil is much improved by the addition of organic material, but a quick boost can also be achieved by adding an organic fertilizer, spreading it over the surface and then raking it lightly in.

RIGHT The acidity of the soil can be reduced by adding lime about a month before planting and working it in with a rake. Check the soil with a soil testing kit to see how much lime is required.

you can still add organic matter to the soil by top-dressing, which simply means spreading the material on the surface. A 10cm/4in layer of, say, farmyard manure will be slowly worked into the soil by the earthworms. As well as being taken into the soil, such a dressing will also act as a mulch, protecting the ground from drying out as well as preventing any annual weed seeds from germinating.

## LEAFMOULD

A natural soil conditioner, leafmould is easy to make and should not cost anything. Only use leafmould made by yourself; never go down to the local woods and help yourself because this will disturb the wood's own cycle.

Four stakes knocked into the ground with some wire-netting stretched around them will make the perfect container for making leafmould. Simply add the leaves as they fall. It will take a couple of years for them to break down, and a huge heap will become a small layer once the process is complete.

Add leafmould to the soil or use it as a top-dressing. It contains few nutrients and is usually acid, so it can help to reduce the pH of alkaline soil. Leafmould from pine needles is particularly acid.

## IMPROVING THE SOIL'S PH

Another aspect of improving soil is to improve the pH level. The level to aim at is pH 6.5, but anything between 6 and 7 is still good, while 5.5–7.5 is acceptable.

If the soil is too acid, the pH can be increased somewhat by adding lime to the soil. Three types of lime can be used for reducing soil acidity. Ordinary lime (calcium carbonate) is the safest to use. Quicklime (calcium oxide) is the strongest and most caustic, but it may cause damage. Slaked lime (calcium hydroxide) is quicklime with water added; it is not as strong as quicklime and is therefore less dangerous. Always take safety precautions when you are applying lime, and follow the quantities recommended by the manufacturer on the packet. Do not add lime at

RIGHT It is best to avoid working on wet soil, but sometimes it is necessary. To ensure that the soil is not compacted and its structure destroyed, it is advisable to work from a plank of wood.

the same time as manure, because this will release ammonia, which can damage plants. Apply the lime over the soil at the rate prescribed on the packet and rake it in. Do not sow or plant in the ground for at least a month. Do not over-lime.

It is not as easy to reduce the alkalinity of soil. Peat (peat moss) used to be recommended for this purpose, but not only is collecting peat environmentally unsound, it breaks down quickly and needs to be constantly replaced. Most organic manures are on the acid side and help to bring down the levels. Leafmould, especially that from pine needles, is also acid.

Spent mushroom compost contains lime, so it is useful for reducing acidity, but it should not be used on alkaline soils.

PLANNING AND PREPARATION  29

# Compost

This is a valuable material for any garden, but it is especially useful in the fruit and vegetable garden. It is free, apart from any capital required in installing compost bins – these should last for many years and the overall cost should be negligible. A little effort is required, but this is a small price to pay for the resulting gold dust.

## THE PRINCIPLE

In making compost, gardeners emulate the natural process in which a plant takes nutrients from the soil, dies and then rots, so the nutrients return to the ground. In the garden, waste plant material is collected, piled in a heap and allowed to rot down before being returned to the soil as crumbly, sweet-smelling, fibrous material.

Because it is kept in a heap, the rotting material generates heat, which encourages it to break down more quickly. The heat also helps to kill pests and diseases, as well as any weed seed in the compost. The balance of air and moisture is important; if the heap is too wet it will go slimy, but if it is too dry it will not decompose. The best balance is achieved by having some ventilation, but protecting the compost from rain, and by using a good mixture of materials.

The process should take up to about three months, but many old-fashioned gardeners like to retain the heap for much longer than that, growing marrows and courgettes (zucchini) on it before they break it up for use in the garden.

## THE COMPOST BIN

Gardeners always seem to generate more garden waste than they ever thought possible and never to have enough compost space, so when planning your bins, make sure you have enough. The overall aim is to have three: one to hold new waste, one that is in the process of breaking down, and a third that is ready for use.

Bins are traditionally made from wood (often scrap wood), and because these can be hand-made to fit your space and the amount of material available, this is still the best option.

LEFT Good compost is dark brown, crumbly and has a sweet, earthy smell, not a rotting one.

ABOVE A range of organic materials can be used, but avoid cooked kitchen waste or any weeds that have seed in them. Clockwise from top left: kitchen waste, weeds, shreddings and grass clippings.

Sheet materials, such as corrugated iron, can also be used. Most ready-made bins are made of plastic, and although these work perfectly well, they may be a bit on the small side in a busy garden.

You can make compost successfully in a bin the size of a dustbin (trash can), but if you have room, one holding a cubic metre/35 cubic feet, or even bigger, will be much more efficient.

The simplest bin can be made by nailing together four wooden pallets to form a box. If the front is made so that the slats are slotted in to form the wall, they can be removed as the bin is emptied, making the job of removing the compost easier.

## MATERIALS

Most garden plant waste can be used for composting, but do not include perennial weeds. Weed seeds will be killed if the compost heats up really well, but it is safest not to include them. You could have a separate bin for anything that contains seeds because the compost can be used for permanent plantings such as trees – if the compost never comes to the surface, seeds will not germinate. Woody material, such as hedge clippings, can be used, but shred it first. Kitchen vegetable waste, such as peelings and cores, can be used, but avoid cooked vegetables and do not include meat, which will attract rats and other vermin.

## TECHNIQUE

Placing a few branches or twiggy material in the bottom of the bin will help to keep the contents aerated. Put in the material as it becomes available, but avoid building up deep layers of any one material, especially grass cuttings. Mix them with other materials.

To help keep the heap warm, cover it with an old carpet or sheet of polythene (plastic). This also prevents excess water from chilling the contents and swamping the air spaces. The lid should be kept on until the compost is needed.

Every so often, add a layer of farmyard manure if you can get it, because it will provide extra nitrogen to speed things up. Failing this, you can buy special compost accelerators. It is not essential to add manure or an accelerator, however – it just means waiting a couple of months longer.

Air is important, and this usually percolates through the side of the bin, so leave a few gaps between the timbers. If you use old pallets, these are usually crudely made, with plenty of gaps. The colder material around the edges takes longer to break down, so turn the compost around every so often. This also loosens the pile and allows air to circulate.

### MAKING COMPOST

**1** To make garden compost, place a layer of "browns" – straw, dry leaves and chipped wood are ideal – into the bin, to a depth of about 15cm/6in.

**2** Begin a layer of "greens" – any green plant material, except perennial or seeding weeds. Fibrous or woody stems should be cut up small or shredded.

**3** Add greens until you have a layer 15cm/6in thick. Mix lawn clippings with other green waste to avoid the layer becoming slimy and airless.

**4** Kitchen refuse, including fruit and vegetable waste and eggshells, can be added, but not cooked or fatty foods. Cover the heap.

**5** Turn the heap occasionally. The speed of composting will vary, but when ready, the compost should be brown, crumbly and sweet-smelling.

# Choosing fruit trees

When choosing which fruit to grow in your garden, consider the position you are intending to plant them in. Select good specimens of reliable and trouble-free varieties that you like to eat.

## BUYING FRUIT TREES

It is important to choose healthy and vigorous specimens when buying fruit trees. Whether you buy bare-root or container-grown plants is a matter of personal preference; most varieties are available as both. Garden centres usually offer a limited range, but for the best choice and for unusual varieties or for trained forms, you will probably find that you need to visit a specialist nursery.

When choosing a fruit tree, look for one with a sturdy, straight main trunk and several well-spaced branches that are not too vertical.

ABOVE An apple tree that has been well cared for and pruned when young will fruit for many years and need little maintenance throughout its life.

### CHOOSING A ROOTSTOCK

Fruit tree varieties are grafted (joined) on to a range of different rootstocks, which vary in their vigour. If you choose a dwarfing rootstock you will get a slower growing, smaller tree while if you choose a vigorous rootstock you will get a much faster growing, larger fruit tree.

Dwarf rootstocks are good for planting in restricted spaces, and produce trees that are easy to manage. For a large tree, choose a vigorous rootstock. Vigorous rootstocks are also worth considering if your soil is very poor, or if the tree will get a lot of competition from surrounding plants.

The rootstocks of apples and pears have been given codes; those of cherries and plums have names.

| Rootstock | Vigour | Eventual size |
|---|---|---|
| **Apples** | | |
| M27 | very dwarf | 1.8m/6ft |
| M9 | dwarf | 2.4m/8ft |
| M26 | semi-dwarf | 3m/10ft |
| MM106 | semi-vigorous | 4.5m/15ft |
| MM111 | vigorous | 5.5m/18ft |
| **Cherries** | | |
| Colt | semi-dwarf | 4.5m/15ft |
| **Pears** | | |
| Quince C | semi-dwarf | 3m/10ft |
| Quince A | semi-vigorous | 3.5m/12ft |
| **Plums** | | |
| Pixy | semi-dwarf | 3m/10ft |
| St Julien A | vigorous | 5.5m/18ft |

This is important because the angle between the branch and the trunk determines how strong the branch will be in later years and, therefore, how much fruit the tree can bear.

Fruit tree varieties are all grafted on to a rootstock, and it is essential that you choose a type to suit your particular needs (see box). It is also important to check that the union between the fruiting variety and rootstock is well healed and strong – look for a bulge about 15cm/6in above the ground. When you buy plum or cherry trees you should also check the branches for rough areas of bark and oozing sap (a sign of canker disease) as well as foliage with a silvery sheen (a sign of silverleaf disease). Avoid suspect plants at all costs.

## CORDONS, FANS AND ESPALIERS

The modern flagpole-type apple varieties grow in a narrow column, and these can be planted almost anywhere within the garden. They require much less watering and attention than ordinary varieties or dwarfing rootstocks grown in pots. In a small garden or confined space, however, by far the best way to grow tree fruits is to train them as a cordon, fan or espalier, against a wall or fence.

Apples, pears and plums can be grown as cordons. A cordon consists of a single stem from which short sideshoots are encouraged to grow out. The main stem is held at an angle of 45 degrees, while the sideshoots are trained along three or four horizontal wires. It is also possible to create cordons with two, three or more main stems, which are trained vertically or at angles. The arcure method involves training the main stem, originally planted at 45 degrees, into a half-circle and, the following year, training another stem from the curve in the opposite direction to form an S-shape. Ultimately, three or four hoops rise above each other.

Fan-trained trees grown against a wall will benefit from the shelter and reflected warmth, and this method is ideal for apricots, greengages, nectarines and peaches. Apples, cherries, pears and plums can also be grown in this way when space is at a premium. The branches are held against horizontal wires, but allowed to radiate outwards from about 60cm/2ft above the ground.

Espaliers are an alternative to cordons and are suitable for apples and pears. Plums and other stone fruits, which do not respond well to hard pruning, do better as fans. An espalier has a central stem from which horizontally trained fruiting arms are trained along wires, usually held at intervals of about 45cm/18in. Step-over espaliers, which have only a single tier of sideshoots, are ideal for edging.

The initial training of cordons, fans and espaliers requires considerable patience. Unless you particularly like the challenge and are prepared to wait for at least two years, buy ready-trained trees.

RIGHT Apple trees can be grown in containers. However, it is essential to water them every day.

ABOVE Cordons are trained at an angle of about 45 degrees, fixed to posts or a fence. Fruit trees grown in this way must be pruned regularly to retain their shape and encourage cropping.

ABOVE Fans can be free-standing, tied to wires supported by posts, but they are usually planted against a wall or fence. In time a fan can be trained to cover a large area, such as a garage wall.

ABOVE Espaliers are similar to cordons except that the branches are trained horizontally. They are often trained against wires fixed to a wall, but they can be free-standing like this example.

# Planting fruit trees

When deciding where to plant fruit trees, think carefully about the size you expect them to reach, and make sure they have enough space. Many are small enough to fit easily into a restricted area, but they do need to receive plenty of sun to ripen the fruit.

## PREPARING THE GROUND

Because most fruit trees are likely to remain in the ground for a long time, it is essential that the soil is thoroughly prepared before planting. If possible, double dig the soil, which means digging down to the depth of two spades. Take care that you do not mix the subsoil with the topsoil. Break up the subsoil and if you garden on very heavy clay, mix in some grit when you return it to the bottom of the hole. Take out all perennial weed roots you notice. It will be impossible to remove these roots once a tree is planted, and they will be certain to regrow, competing with the young tree for moisture and nutrients. If possible, leave the ground fallow for a month or two so that you can hoe off any annual weeds that germinate.

Once you have removed the weeds, add plenty of well-rotted organic material to the soil as you dig. This will not only help keep the soil moist but will also provide a continuous supply of nutrients – water, especially, is crucial while the tree is young. Once it is established, the roots will be able to reach further to find the nutrients and water the plant needs. After the tree has been planted, organic material will have to be applied to the soil's surface and left for the worms to take down to the roots.

## PLANTING

As long as the weather is neither too wet nor too cold, the best time to plant fruit trees is between late autumn and mid-spring. If bare-rooted plants are delivered when the ground is water-logged or frozen, heel them in temporarily – that is, plant them leaning over, almost horizontal – until conditions are suitable for planting. Container-grown plants can be planted at other times of the year, but they are likely to need a lot more watering.

Fruit trees and bushes should be planted to the same depth as they were in their pots or nursery bed when you purchased them.

### PREPARING TO PLANT

**1** Make sure the ground is free of weeds and incorporate well-rotted compost or manure. Excavate a hole at least one-third wider than the tree's container (the bigger the better), and fork over the bottom so that the plant does not sit on compacted ground.

**2** Mix a couple of buckets of well-rotted organic material with excavated soil, also adding a handful of slow release fertilizer to the mixture. Soak the rootball in water. Remove the tree from its container and gently tease out any roots that have spiralled around the rootball so that they will grow outwards once planted.

If a tree needs staking, place the stake in the ground before planting. Water the plants in thoroughly and keep them watered in dry weather until they are firmly established. Apply a mulch around the base of the plant in order to help preserve moisture as well as to keep the weeds down. Remove any weeds that do appear.

## LABELLING

Try to keep a record of what you have planted. Fruit trees often outlive any label that comes with them, and it is often annoying when asked for the variety of an apple, for example, when you cannot remember. A notebook with details of the variety and where you purchased the plant, as well as the date on which you planted it, will be of future interest.

## PLANTING THE TREE

**1** Place the tree in the hole to check that the hole is deep enough. Use a straight edge to make sure that the original growing compost surface is level with the surrounding ground.

**2** After teasing out the roots, place the tree in the hole, holding it while you fill around it with soil, to make sure that it is upright and at the correct depth. Firm the soil in well to hold it in place.

**3** If putting the stake in after planting, do it at an angle to avoid damaging the roots. It should be at the windward side (where the wind mostly blows from) to prevent chafing. Saw off any excess.

**4** Tie the tree to the stake using a tree tie. Nail it to the stake – not the tree – using a flat-headed nail, and do not hammer it in fully.

**5** As the tree grows, remove the nail and loosen the tie. Remove the stake after a year; longer staking can result in weak stem growth. Saw the stake off at ground level to avoid disturbing the roots.

# Supporting fruit trees

Once they are established, most free-standing fruit trees will need no support. Trees trained in fans or as cordons or espaliers, however, need a permanent framework of wires against which they can be trained. Because the wires will carry a considerable weight, they must be firmly supported, whether they are fixed to a wall or fence or held on secure stakes to provide a middle-of-the-border feature.

### INDIVIDUAL SUPPORTS

A tree needs a stake when it is first planted, especially if it is in an exposed position. Once it has developed a good root system, however, it will do better if the stake is removed.

The stake should be inserted before the tree is planted so that there is no danger that the roots will be damaged when the stake is driven into position. Although it is important that the stake is knocked securely into the ground, only 45–50cm/18–20in need show above ground. Recent practice is to support trees quite low down, at about 30cm/1ft above the ground, so that the lower part of the tree and, most importantly, the rootball are held firmly in place while the upper part can move freely in the wind, gaining strength as it does so.

Tie the tree to the stake, using a buckle-and-spacer tree tie that will provide good support but at the same time not cut into or chafe the trunk. If you use a simple rubber or plastic tie, which does not have a buckle, nail the tie to the stake so that it does not move about and rub the bark. It is important to check the tie at least twice a year to make sure that it is still secure, and at the same time to make sure that it is not too tight and cutting into the bark.

If a tree that is already in position needs staking, place the stake at an angle to the trunk (facing into the prevailing wind) so that it enters the ground at some distance from the base of the tree to avoid damaging the roots. Alternatively, drive in two stakes, each some distance from the tree and on opposite sides of the trunk. Then you can either fix a cross-bar to the stakes and tie the tree to the cross-bar or use two heavy-duty rubber ties, one for each stake, to hold the tree.

### WALL AND FENCE FRUIT

Several types of fruit trees can be trained flat against walls or fences, and these can be very decorative. These plants will need some means of holding them against the wall, and this usually takes the form of

### ERECTING FREE-STANDING WIRE SUPPORTS

**1** Knock a stout post firmly into the ground at the end of the row. An alternative is to dig a hole and insert the post before refilling and ramming down the earth.

**2** Knock another post at a 45 degree angle to the vertical to act as a support to the upright post. Nail it firmly so that the upright post is rigid and will not be pulled over by tight wires.

**3** Fasten the wire around one end post and pull tight along the row, stapling it to each post. Keep the wire as taut as possible. If necessary, use eye-bolts on the end posts to tension the wire.

wires. To make sure that the framework lasts as long as possible use a galvanized wire, which will not corrode. The wire is held in place by vine eyes, of which there are two main types available. Some are flat, metal spikes, which are hammered into the mortar between the bricks, while others are screw eyes, which are screwed into wall plugs that have been inserted into holes in the brick or stonework of the wall. They can be screwed directly into wooden fences. The eyes are placed 60–90cm/2–3ft apart and a wire led through the hole in each one. The wire is secured at the end eyes by pulling it back and twisting it around itself or by using a tensioning screw that can be tightened to tension the wire. The wires should be parallel to each other and 30–45cm/12–18in apart.

## SUPPORTING A TREE AGAINST A WALL

1 To support trees against walls, use wires held by vine eyes. Depending on the type of vine eye, either knock them into the wall or drill and plug holes before screwing them in.

2 Pass galvanized wire through the holes in the eyes and fasten to the end ones, keeping the wire as tight as possible or using a tensioner at one end of each wire.

BELOW Cordons take up so little space that you can have many varieties in a small garden, and because they can be trained against a fence or wall, they do not have to encroach on other valuable growing space.

ABOVE The branches of small apple trees can be trained to spread by tying them down with string tied to the trunk.

PLANNING AND PREPARATION 37

# Pruning

Many gardeners are confused about pruning, but it is not really difficult – the main thing is knowing when to do it, and how much to remove. While failing to prune at all may not cause serious damage, it will certainly not make for the most healthy and productive trees, and they may also become too large. More serious damage can be caused by pruning at the wrong time, or in the wrong way, which may even occasionally be fatal to the tree.

## PRUNING CUTS

Although different fruit trees and styles of training involve different pruning methods, the pruning cuts are the same in all instances. Use sharp secateurs (pruners), loppers or a pruning knife and make sure you are comfortably positioned to make a clean, neat cut. If you need to stand on a ladder, either make sure that someone will hold it for you or use one of the special garden ladders that has an integral stabilizer.

Always cut a stem just above a bud and make sure that the cut is angled away from the bud. Do not cut too far above the bud, or the stem will die back, possibly allowing disease to enter the tissue; do not cut too close to the bud or you may damage it, which will prevent it from growing properly and may encourage disease.

Branches that are large enough to be cut with a saw are usually cut across at right angles. If the branch is heavy and thick and likely to break, thereby splitting the wood before the cut is complete, the sawing is usually done in three separate stages. The first cut is made on the underside of the branch, 5cm/2in out from the final cutting position. The second cut is made slightly further out along the branch, this time from above, by sawing down until the branch splits along to the first cut and is then severed. The final cut can be made straight through from the top because there is no weight to cause splitting.

## PRUNING TIMES

When apples and pears are grown as standards or half-standards they are pruned in winter. When grown as espaliers and cordons they are usually pruned in both winter and summer. Winter pruning is usually carried out during the tree's dormancy (between leaf-fall and bud-burst), but it can be done when the buds have begun to swell. Delayed winter pruning can, however, check subsequent growth, although it can be used to advantage to keep a too-vigorous tree under control.

Plums, greengages, damsons and cherries grown as standards need little or no pruning beyond

ABOVE When pruning a dwarf bush apple, start by keeping the centre of the tree open and uncongested. Remove congested or crossing branches by carefully cutting them back to their point of origin.

ABOVE Spur pruning is an easy technique suitable for most apple varieties. Unless your apple is one of the rare tip-bearers, shorten the previous summer's growth on the main shoots on each branch by two-thirds to three-quarters. If the shoot grew 60cm/2ft last summer, shorten it to leave about 15–20cm/6–8in. On a large tree, cut some back to within one or two buds.

the removal in spring of crossing, rubbing or dead branches. When they are trained as fans against a wall, misplaced shoots are removed in spring to midsummer. To avoid silverleaf, plums, greengages, damsons and cherries are pruned only when the sap is rising.

Peaches and nectarines can be pruned in spring when training against a wall, and again after harvesting. Pruning should encourage the plant to produce shoots to replace those that have borne fruits. Apricots should be pruned after harvesting, and at the same time, shoots that are needed to fill the spaces should be tied into place while they are still flexible.

## PRUNING CORDONS

**1** On cordons, prune any sideshoots that are more than 10cm/4in long, shortening them to about 5cm/2in. If there are none, do not worry.

**2** Once the main stem has reached the top wire, prune back the tip to within 12–25mm/½–1in of the old wood. Repeat annually wih any new leaders that form.

## GOOD AND BAD PRUNING CUTS

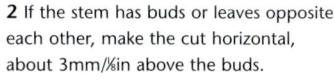

**1** A good pruning cut is made about 3mm/⅛in above a strong bud. It should be a slanting cut, with the higher end above the bud, and the cut sloping by about 45 degrees. The bud should generally be facing outward from the plant rather than inward; the latter will throw its shoot into the plant, crossing and rubbing against other stems, which should be avoided. This is an easy technique, and you can practise it on any tree, bush or shrub.

**2** If the stem has buds or leaves opposite each other, make the cut horizontal, about 3mm/⅛in above the buds.
**3** Do not use blunt secateurs (pruners). These will produce a ragged or bruised cut, which is likely to introduce disease into the plant.
**4** Do not cut too far above a bud. The piece of stem above the bud is likely to die back and the stem may well die back even further down, possibly causing the loss of the whole stem.

**5** Do not cut too close to the bud, otherwise the bud might be damaged by the secateurs, distorting growth or allowing disease to enter. Too close a cut is likely to cause the stem to die back to the next bud.

**6** It is bad practice to slope the cut towards the bud because this makes the stem above the bud too long, which is likely to cause dieback. It also sheds rain on to the bud, which may cause rot and allow disease to enter.

PLANNING AND PREPARATION

# Protecting fruit

Gardeners are not the only animals to like fruit. Many others – birds in particular – do so as well, and the only way to make sure that there is enough left for the gardener to enjoy is to protect the fruit trees in some way. The only practical way to do this is to put some form of physical barrier between the predators and the fruit.

## FRUIT CAGES

There is no doubt that the easiest way to protect fruit is with a complete cage. The advantages of this are that it covers the area completely and that the gardener can walk around within it, maintaining the trees or harvesting the fruit. When protection is provided for individual trees, each cover has to be removed in turn, which can be tiresome, especially if netting snags on branches.

The only problem with caging on a large scale is that it can be expensive. If you have every intention of leaving the fruit cage where it is, it might be more economical in the long term to build a cage with long-lasting materials. Use thick posts and make the covering from fine-mesh galvanized wire netting which, although more expensive than plastic, will outlive replacements of its plastic equivalent.

Ready-made fruit cages are expensive but they still probably work out cheaper than making one of your own, unless, of course, you have access to free materials, such as posts. Fruit cages are supplied in kit form and are easy to erect; they can usually be ordered to whatever size you require. Make sure that there are no gaps in the netting and that it is well pegged down or buried at the base because birds have a knack of finding the smallest hole to squeeze through.

A home-made fruit cage is time-consuming to construct, but you can make it fit any shape and cover any area you want. Metal posts, such as scaffolding poles, will last forever, but most gardeners find that wooden poles are more practical. They should be sturdy and treated at their base with preservative. Each should be let into the ground by about 60cm/ 24in for security, because the netting will act as a sail, putting great pressure on the posts in strong winds.

The covering can be plastic netting, but galvanized wire netting will last longer and be less likely to tear accidentally. Some gardeners like to remove the top covering to allow birds to eat pests when the fruit is not actually ripening, and if you want to do this, use wire sides and a plastic netting for the top. Another reason for being able to remove the top covering in winter, especially if it is plastic, is that the weight of a heavy fall of snow can stretch and break it. The tops of the poles are best covered with a smooth, rounded object, and although it may look ugly, it will prevent the plastic netting from being chafed and worn as the wind moves it against the posts.

LEFT A fruit cage is expensive but it is the only really effective way of protecting fruit from birds.

RIGHT Fruit trees and bushes trained against a wall or fence can be protected with a home-made frame, as seen here. A similar frame can be covered with horticultural fleece to protect the blossom from frosts.

## WALL-TRAINED PLANTS

When a fruit tree is grown against a wall as a fan-trained specimen or as a cordon or espalier, it can be easier to provide protection for it than in the open garden. A temporary screen against birds can be provided by supporting fine mesh on canes. When the danger has passed, the canes can be simply moved out of the way. Similarly, horticultural fleece can be used in winter to protect tender plants from frosts.

A more permanent framework can be created from wooden battens nailed to the wall so that the plastic net or wire netting can be held well away from the plant. Wire mesh should be used with caution because condensation drops from the galvanizing can lead to zinc toxicity.

If you grow peaches, nectarines or apricots outdoors, one of the most troublesome diseases is peach leaf curl, a fungal disease that causes blisters on the leaves, which turn white and then drop. The fungal spores are transferred by water droplets, and one of the best ways of protecting wall-trained plants is to erect a frame from which a plastic sheet can be suspended from early winter to early summer. The sheet must be held away from the leaves and blossom, and the covering should be open at each end to allow air to circulate freely.

LEFT These pole apples have been grown as vertical cordons. The bottoms of the trunks have been protected against attacks by rabbits.

PLANNING AND PREPARATION   41

# Harvesting and storing

The best fruit is always the crop you pick and pop straight into your mouth. Given kind weather and a certain amount of skill on the gardener's part, however, there should be sufficient fruit not only to eat immediately but also to store for later use.

## HARVESTING

Fruit should be properly ripe before it is harvested for immediate use. There is little point in picking it early and leaving it to ripen – it will always ripen better on the tree. Fruit for storing should be mature and ripe – but do not pick at the very peak of ripeness; instead aim for just a little before. This is a matter of judgement and will come with experience. The time to pick is when the fruit comes away easily in the hand.

ABOVE Apples are removed with a twist of the wrist.

Apples, for example, will come free with a gentle grip and a little twist of the wrist.

To make sure that the fruit you pick is completely ripe, it is usually necessary to make several passes over a tree, taking only the fruits that come away easily and beginning with the side of the tree that receives the most sun. Always pick fruit when it is dry.

Never pick an apple without a stalk, which will leave a hole through which rot can enter, and take care that you do not bruise the flesh, which will also lead to rot.

Pears are even more delicate than apples and must be picked with the greatest care so that they are not bruised or damaged. Make sure that the stalk is intact. Pick pears before they ripen fully because they will taste better if they are left for a day or two before being eaten. If they are harvested too early, however, they may shrivel.

Plums will be ready for harvesting at any time from midsummer to late autumn, depending on the variety. Not all the fruit on a tree will ripen at the same time, and several passes over a tree will be necessary. Make sure the stalk is intact. Plums do not keep well, but if they are a little underripe when they are picked, they will keep in a cool place for up to a fortnight. Plums and damsons that are destined for jam, cooking or bottling should be rather underripe.

### HOW TO STORE

Apples and pears can be stored in a cool place for up to 12 months, depending on the variety. Fruits can also be preserved by bottling or making into jam. These are among the best ways to store some of the most popular fruits. There are, of course, variations on the methods suggested and if in doubt you should consult an authoritative cookbook.

**Apples:** store wrapped; freeze as slices or purée; bottle as slices
**Apricots:** freeze halved; bottle
**Cherries:** freeze after stoning (pitting); bottle
**Peaches and nectarines:** freeze soon after stoning – they discolour quickly; bottle after stoning
**Pears:** store wrapped
**Plums and damsons:** freeze after stoning; bottle

Cherries, too, should always be picked with the stalk still attached, and this is most easily done with secateurs (pruners) or scissors. Do not pull the cherry from the stalk; if the stalk is left hanging, it might allow rot to enter the tree. Leave the cherries on the tree until they are perfectly ripe, unless they show signs of cracking, in which case they should be picked immediately.

Peaches and nectarines are ripe when the skin begins to be flushed with red and the fruit feels just soft at the stalk end. The fruit should come away easily from the tree.

Depending on the variety, apricots can be ready for harvesting any time from midsummer to early

LEFT Apples and pears can be stored in trays in a cool place. Make sure the fruits are not touching each other, so that if one rots it will not infect the others.

autumn, and they are ripe about a week after the fruit stops swelling. Take care that you do not damage the skin as you pick them, and harvest them with the stalk intact.

Citrus fruits should be picked as they ripen. In the right conditions, the fruits will reach a good size before they begin to colour. Use secateurs to remove the fruit from the plant and take care that you do not damage the skin.

## STORING

Only apples and pears can be kept for any length of time after picking without some form of preservation, and it is worth bearing in mind that some varieties keep better than others. 'Cox's Orange Pippin' apples, for example, can be kept until spring, but 'Beauty of Bath' apples should be eaten straight away because they do not last much longer than a week. In general, early-maturing apples do not store, but later ones do.

Keep only fruits that are in perfect condition. Discard any that are marked, bruised or showing signs of rot. Apples and pears should be stored in a draught-free, frost-proof place, such as a shed, garage or cellar, from which bright light can be excluded. The temperature should ideally be under 45°C/7°F and fairly constant. Take the fruit into the house only as it is needed because the higher temperature will cause it to deteriorate.

It is often recommended that apples and pears be wrapped in newspaper before being stored. However, checking stored fruit for rot involves unwrapping each fruit, and it is far more efficient if the fruit can be laid in trays or racks, with pieces of card or paper separating the individual fruits. This ensures that fruits do not touch each other and makes it easier to check the fruit regularly for signs of rot.

### FREEZING AND PRESERVING

The modern way of preserving fruit is freezing. Pears and apples can be frozen, but it is best to slice them or even cook and purée them before freezing. Plums and damsons can also be frozen; remove the stones first. Stone fruits are also often bottled, and other more traditional methods include drying, which is ideal for apricots and is also sometimes used for apples and pears.

ABOVE Citrus fruits such as oranges, lemons and grapefruit can be preserved by cooking them in sugar and water to make marmalade.

# Pests and diseases

Although there are many pests and diseases that can affect fruit trees, and some gardeners become very worried about them, most of the time they do not cause serious harm. Often the problem is not as bad as it looks, and can be contained without the use of chemical deterrents.

### ANIMALS
There is one type of pest that is very difficult to control: mammals. They can rarely be killed and are difficult to deter. The only really effective action that you can take is to build a barricade around your garden. Wire netting, which will keep out most animals, should be partially buried in the ground to prevent burrowing species, such as rabbits, getting underneath. For the more athletic species, such as deer, the barrier will need to be at least 2.4m/8ft high if you are to prevent them from jumping over it. Fortunately, there is no need to resort to such measures unless you live in an area where these pests are a problem. You will rarely be troubled if you garden in a town.

ABOVE An apple that has been damaged by codling moth. The caterpillars make tunnels through the fruit, spoiling it and sometimes causing it to drop prematurely before ripening.

### BIRDS
Bird scarers can be used, but although they are effective in the short term, birds soon get used to them. Chemical repellents are also available, but these quickly wash off in wet weather and in very cold spells, when birds are hungry, will not be effective anyway. Netting draped over individual trees is effective but is difficult to put on and remove if you do not have help. Black cotton (never nylon) thread strung between branches is also a good deterrent, but is time-consuming to put in place.

If you have only a small crop, it is worth protecting individual fruits or clusters of fruit with muslin, paper or perforated plastic bags, and cardboard collars fastened immediately above ripening fruits will stop birds getting close enough to peck the fruit.

### INSECTS
Apples and pears are susceptible to damage from codling moths, the caterpillars of which eat into the fruit and are usually not noticed until the fruit is cut open. Regular spraying will control the caterpillars, but blue tits, if you can encourage them, are more efficient.

Many types of caterpillar, feeding in spring, will damage buds, leaves and blossom. Sticky greasebands placed around tree trunks from autumn to spring will trap the wingless winter moths that

ABOVE Damage to bark by rabbits can be prevented by using wire guards.

ABOVE The dark blotches on these apple leaves indicate an attack of the fungal disease silverleaf. To prevent the disease spreading, limit pruning to summer only. Vigorous growth during this period helps to prevent the disease from gaining entry through pruning cuts.

are largely responsible. The caterpillars of sawflies, which damage plums and apples, causing early fruit drop, can be controlled by spraying.

In recent years the range of insecticides available to amateur gardeners has been reduced as regulatory authorities have recognized the long-term dangers inherent in chemical residues. If you feel that an insecticide is the only effective way of dealing with a pest, make sure that it is not one that has been lurking in your shed for several years. Use formulations that are designed to control the particular pest – it is no good using something that will kill aphids if your problem is codling moth – and always follow the manufacturer's instructions to the letter.

## DISEASES

The worst diseases likely to affect fruit trees are canker, silverleaf, scab and peach leaf curl. Apples and pears are susceptible to canker, which causes sunken, discoloured patches, from which slime oozes. Cut out and burn infected branches and spray with a fungicide. Badly affected trees should be removed and burned.

Silverleaf is a serious fungal disease, especially of plums, and there is no chemical cure. The leaves turn silvery, then brown, and it causes progressive dieback of branches. If fungal growths are seen on the trunk, dig up and burn the entire tree. Otherwise, cut back branches at least 15cm/6in behind the infected tissue.

Scab, which affects apples and pears, can be seen on the fruit, but also affects the leaves, which fall prematurely. Remove and burn all fallen leaves and spray regularly.

Peach leaf curl, a fungal problem also affecting apricots and nectarines, causes the leaves to blister, turn white and drop. Remove and burn infected leaves and spray with a fungicide. Protect wall-trained and container plants from rain early in the year.

Pears and, less often, apples can be affected by fireblight, which causes shoots to die back and the foliage to wither, turn brown and drop. Cut back shoots at least 30cm/12in behind the infected tissue. When entire plants show symptoms, dig them up and burn them. Disinfect your pruning saw and secateurs (pruners) after use.

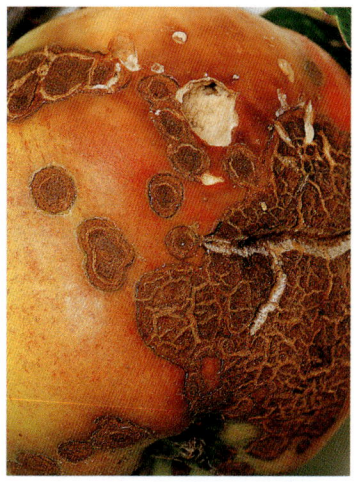

ABOVE Apple scab is a fungal disease that is spread by wind and rain. Fruit develops dark patches and leaves show brown or green blotches. Pruning can prevent the disease as it helps maintain good air circulation. Cut out and burn affected twigs.

RIGHT Biological controls are an increasingly successful way to fight pests. They are mainly used in greenhouses, but others are now becoming available for the open garden. The control insects are released, here from a sachet, in order to attack the pests.

# Growing tree fruit organically

As increasing numbers of people become concerned about the levels of artificial insecticides, fungicides and weedkillers used in the commercial production of fruit, the attractions of organically grown produce are becoming ever more self-evident.

### ORGANIC GARDENS
There is more to organic gardening than just not using chemicals. Organic gardeners work to improve the quality of the soil to provide plants with the best possible growing conditions. They also aim to develop a natural balance within the garden by attracting wildlife to help combat pests and to pollinate plants, and by growing a wide range of plants. In this way, attacks by pests and diseases are likely to affect only a small proportion of the fruit garden.

### COMPANION PLANTING
As well as sometimes referring to the practice of growing different types of plants mixed together, to lessen the danger of an entire crop being wiped out by a pest or disease, "companion planting" specifically means planting certain beneficial plants alongside crops that are being grown. Chives, for example, can deter scab and aphids, though you need to plant a large area, not just one or two plants. Many open, daisy-like flowers will attract hoverflies, whose larvae prey on aphids. Among the most effective are the poached-egg plant (*Limnanthes douglasii*), pot marigold (*Calendula officinalis*) and alpine strawberries.

ABOVE Growing flowers alongside fruit and vegetables is an increasingly popular idea, especially when limited space makes it difficult to have a dedicated kitchen garden. As well as looking good, these sunflowers will attract birds, which will help to control insects.

### FEEDING THE SOIL
As organic gardeners do not use chemical fertilizers, nutrients need to be added to the soil in organic forms. Garden compost and well-rotted manure are among the most useful, and these and other bulky organic materials have the added advantage of improving the texture of the soil.

### VEGETABLE INDUSTRIAL WASTE
Several industries produce organic waste material that can be useful in the garden. Spent hop waste from the brewing industry has always been a favourite among those who can obtain it. Cocoa shells are now imported, although these are better used as a mulch than as a soil conditioner. Several other products are locally available. Allow them to rot well before using.

### PEAT
Although peat has been used in gardens for a long time, its use as a soil improver is to be discouraged. This is partly because removal of peat from the wild is damaging to the environment and partly because it has little nutritional value and breaks down too quickly in the soil to be of much use.

## BENEFICIAL PREDATORS IN THE GARDEN

**Hoverflies**: Their larvae eat aphids. They can be encouraged into the garden by planting daisy-flowered or other open-flowered species.
**Lacewings**: The larvae eat practically all pests during their development. Attract them by erecting "lacewing hotels" in mid- to late summer.
**Ladybirds**: Adults and larvae eat aphids.
*Cryptolaemus montrouzieri*: Native to Australia, this has been used for decades to control mealybug infestations in citrus crops.
**Tachinid flies**: The larvae parasitize other insect hosts, especially caterpillars. They can be attracted in the same way as hoverflies.

## BENEFICIAL PREDATORS

Organic gardeners usually spend a lot of time and effort trying to attract birds into their gardens. Enormous numbers of aphids, wasps and caterpillars will be eaten in the course of a year by birds visiting a garden – it has been estimated, for example, that blue tits can account for more than 90 per cent of codling moth cocoons. Unfortunately, however, birds are extremely fond of fruit. Bullfinches can completely strip the overwintering buds from plum, greengage and cherry trees, and blackbirds, thrushes and starlings can do considerable damage to ripening crops. It is important to strike a balance between protecting plants when they are vulnerable and encouraging birds that prey on insect pests.

Biological controls are increasingly used to control many common pests, although some are not suitable for outdoor use. Among the most useful is *Bacillus thuringiensis*, a bacterium that prevents caterpillars from eating, thereby effectively killing them. Its increasing use in genetically modified corn is, unfortunately, making it less effective in the US, where resistant varieties of pests have developed. It is still worth using in UK gardens, however.

Introduce biological controls as soon as the first signs of attack are noticed. Be patient and accept that there will be some damage before the biological agent takes effect – there will always be some pests, which are essential for the predator to continue to breed, but the population will be reduced.

ABOVE A "lacewing hotel" provides an area where lacewings – which prey on aphids, larvae, mites and thrips – can live.

LEFT Here, the flowers are situated close enough to the fruit and vegetables to become an integrated part of the potager.

PLANNING AND PREPARATION

# Tools and equipment

If you look in the average garden centre you would imagine that you need a tremendous battery of tools and equipment before you could ever consider gardening, but in fact you can start (and continue) gardening with relatively few tools and no equipment at all.

## BUYING TOOLS

It is not necessary to buy a vast armoury of tools when you first start gardening. Most of the jobs can be done with a basic kit. When you are buying tools, always choose the best you can afford. Try forks and spades for size so that you do not strain your back. Many of the cheaper ones are made of pressed steel, which soon becomes blunt and will often bend. Stainless steel is undoubtedly the best, but it tends to be expensive. Ordinary steel implements can be almost as good, especially if you keep them clean. Avoid tools that are made of aluminium. Trowels and hand forks especially are often made of aluminium, but they wear down and blunt quickly and are not good value for money.

A good pair of secateurs (pruners) will be essential for cutting back the branches of fruit trees and bushes. The two most popular types are bypass and anvil secateurs. Bypass secateurs have a sharpened, convex blade, which cuts against a broad concave or straight blade. As long the blades are sharp, this type of secateurs cuts cleanly and is useful for getting into small corners.

Anvil secateurs have a straight blade that cuts against a flat anvil, which may have a groove cut in it to allow sap to run away. The anvil is made of softer metal than the cutting blade to reduce the blunting effect. If you do not keep the cutting blade sharp, this type of secateurs tends to crush the stem rather than cutting it cleanly, and this can lead to pests or diseases entering the plant's tissues.

Some secateurs have a ratchet device built in, which is useful if you find ordinary secateurs difficult to work with. The ratchet makes it possible to cut a stem in several small movements, which require less effort than a single cut.

> **SOIL TESTERS**
>
> A range of products are available for testing different aspects of soil quality. The most common checks the pH (acidity/alkalinity). Some types involve mixing soil samples with a chemical; with others, you insert a metal wand into the soil and read the result on a meter.

## CARE AND MAINTENANCE

Look after your tools. If you do this they will not only always be in tip-top working condition but should last for many years. Scrape all the mud and vegetation off the tools as soon as you have used them. Once they are clean, run an oily rag lightly over the metal parts. The thin film of oil will stop the metal from corroding. This not only helps the tools to last longer but also makes them easier to use – less effort is needed to use a clean spade than one that has a rough, rusty surface.

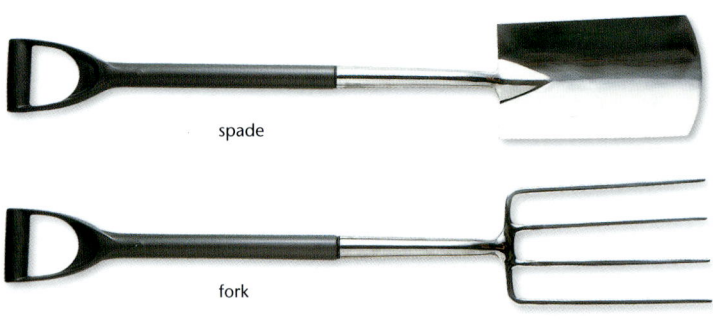

spade

fork

trowel

hand fork

gloves

## LABELLING AND TYING

When working in the garden, it is useful to have a tray of odds and ends, such as scissors, string, raffia, plant ties, labels and marker pens. It is always best to label plants immediately so that you do not forget what you have planted and where it is located.

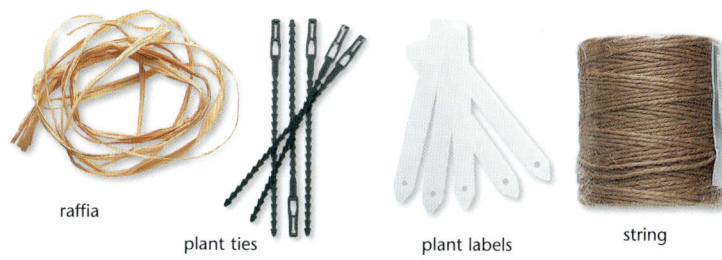

raffia

plant ties

plant labels

string

## EQUIPMENT

It is possible to maintain a fruit garden with no mechanical aids at all. Perhaps the only mechanical device that you may require is a rotavator (rototiller), which is used for digging and breaking up the soil, especially if you want to break down a heavy soil into a fine tilth. This can be useful if your garden is overgrown. All mechanical equipment should be maintained in good working order, and make sure you always follow the safety instructions, as equipment can often be dangerous if used carelessly.

In addition, keep the wooden parts of tools clean, wiping them over with linseed oil if the wood becomes too dry. Keep all blades sharp and hang up tools in a dry place if possible to prevent corrosion. Standing spades and hoes on the ground, especially if it is concrete, will blunt them over time. Always keep all tools away from children.

knife

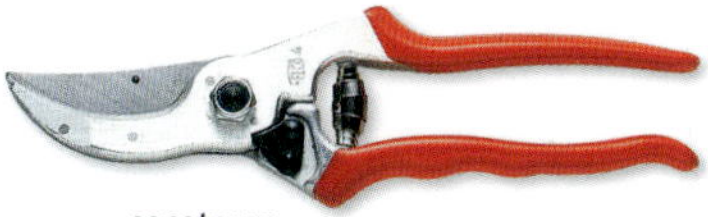

secateurs (pruners)

pruning saw

soil test meter

push, plate or Dutch hoe

draw hoe or swan-neck hoe

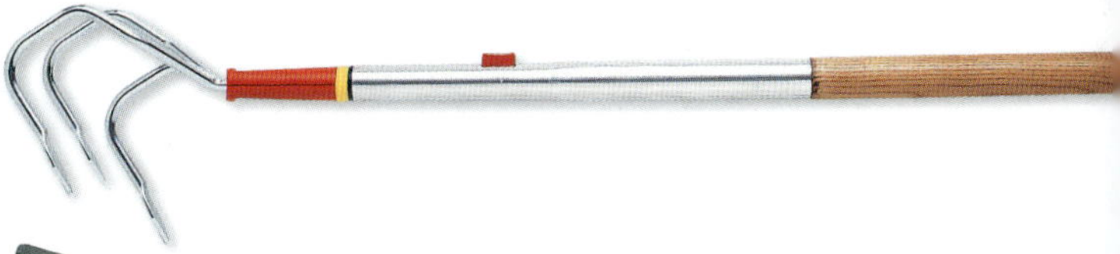

cultivator

rake

PLANNING AND PREPARATION   49

# cultivating tree fruit

You do not need a large garden to grow a few fruit trees. It is possible to train trees against walls and fences or use them as garden dividers, and there are even dwarf forms of popular fruits that are small enough to grow in containers. Established fruit trees are able to compete with other plants for moisture and nutrients, and so can be accommodated all around the garden. Make sure they are planted in a sunny spot and that there is sufficient access to carry out essential maintenance. If you want to grow a lot of fruit, you should consider allocating a separate area of the garden where the fruit trees are easier to manage and protect.

# Growing apples

One aspect of apple growing that may restrict your choice is pollination. Most apples need another variety to pollinate them, and because the flowering time varies from variety to variety, it is essential to choose two that flower during the same period.

Another question that will have to be addressed is the type of plant you want. Standard trees look best and produce a heavy crop, but they are usually too large for today's smaller garden, and ladders are needed for pruning and harvesting. Cordons take up the least space, and although the crop is small, cordons allow you to have several different varieties in a small space.

## CULTIVATION

Apple trees will be in position for years, so prepare the soil well, adding plenty of organic material. An open, sunny position is best. Plant young trees at any time between late autumn and early spring when weather and soil conditions are favourable. The planting distances vary considerably depending on the type and size of tree. Cordons may be only 75cm/30in apart, but the full standards can be 10m/30ft or more apart. Stake young trees, especially if they are in a windy position. Newly planted trees should not be allowed to dry out. Mulch around the tree every spring with organic material. If necessary, protect the blossom from late frosts with fleece.

SPUR PRUNING AN APPLE BUSH TREE
After planting, cut back the leader to about 75cm/30in above the ground. Leave any sideshoots that appear just below this cut and remove any others lower down. The following year, reduce all new growth by about half. This will form the basic framework. Subsequent pruning is restricted to reducing the length of new growth by about a third and removing overcrowded growth.

> **ROOTSTOCKS**
>
> The rootstock on an apple tree affects the size and rate of growth of the tree.
> **M27**: an extreme dwarfing stock (bush, dwarf pyramid, cordon)
> **M9**: dwarfing stock (bush, dwarf pyramid, cordon)
> **M26**: semi-dwarfing stock (bush, dwarf pyramid, cordon)
> **MM106**: semi-dwarfing stock (bush, spindle bush, cordon, fan, espalier)
> **M7**: semi-dwarfing stock (bush, spindle bush, cordon, fan, espalier)
> **M4**: semi-vigorous stock (bush, spindle bush)
> **MM4**: vigorous stock (standard)
> **M2**: vigorous stock
> **MM111**: vigorous stock (half-standard, standard, large bush, large fan, large espalier)
> **M25**: vigorous stock (standard)
> **MM109**: vigorous stock
> **M1**: vigorous stock

LEFT Once an espaliered apple tree has reached its final height, cut the main stem back to a bud just above the top wire. Future growth will be directed into the horizontal branches.

ABOVE The sight of apples, ripening in the late summer sunshine, will inspire even the most faint-hearted of gardeners.

ABOVE Training cordon apples against a fence in this way is a suitable method of growing fruit if you have a small garden.

Thin the apples in early and midsummer if there are too many of them left after the "June drop"; a good guide is to ensure that individual fruits should not touch each other. If branches begin to sag under the weight of fruit, the fruit may need thinning or you may need to support the branches so that they do not break.

## PRUNING AND TRAINING

Most apple trees produce fruit on spurs found on older wood; these can be pruned as described opposite and below. With tip-bearing types, shorten any sideshoots longer than 23cm/9in, which do not have a fruiting bud at the tip (these are rounder and fatter than growth buds), cutting them back to 5–6 buds in spring. Most training and pruning involves cutting out dead or weak wood and maintaining the shape and open nature of the tree. Larger trees are pruned in winter only, but those with a more controlled shape need to be pruned in both winter and summer.

## HARVESTING AND STORAGE

Apples should be picked when ripe, which is usually when the fruit comes away easily with a quick twist of the wrist. Some apples store better than others; in general, early apples do not store as well as later ones. If possible, store in a dark, dry, cool place, and ensure that the fruits do not touch.

## PESTS AND DISEASES

A wide range of pests and diseases can affect the trees and fruit. Birds, wasps and codling moths are three of the most important pests. Canker is one of the worst diseases, but trees may also be affected by scab and mildew.

PLANTING AND PRUNING AN APPLE CORDON Cordons are planted as feather maidens at 45 degrees to the wirework. All sideshoots are cut back to three buds on planting. Subsequent summer pruning (above right) consists of cutting back any new sideshoots to three leaves and new growth on existing sideshoots to one leaf. Winter pruning consists of thinning out any of the older spurs if they have become congested.

CULTIVATING TREE FRUIT

# Growing pears

In the past, pears were grown not just for eating raw, but often for cooking or making perry, a drink akin to cider. Pears for cooking and perry did not have to be the luscious juicy ones that are wanted for eating, and so many people have inherited trees in their gardens that bear pears that are as hard as bullets. This, unfortunately, has put them off growing pears altogether, which is a shame, because ripe eating pears can be mouth-watering.

Pears can be grown as standard or dwarf trees as well as in the form of cordons, espaliers and fans. For the smaller garden, cordons are ideal as they make it possible to have several different varieties in a relatively small area, which means that you can spread the harvest over a longer period. Pears need warmth to grow well, which is one reason why they are frequently grown against a wall. The warmth is needed not only during the spring at blossom time – they are particularly susceptible to frosts – but also in summer and autumn so that the fruit can ripen properly. In cold years, when the pears remain hard, they can still be cooked to make them soft and edible.

Pear trees, when grown on their own rootstocks, are too vigorous for growing in the smaller forms – they will make a large tree. It is more usual to grow a pear tree that has been grafted on to a quince rootstock to curb its vigour. This means that any suckers appearing below the graft should be removed.

As with apples, pears must be grown near a different variety so that the blossom can be pollinated. Unless there is a compatible tree nearby, you will have to plant at least two trees. Unfortunately, you cannot use any variety – they must be compatible. Consult your supplier about suitable pairs.

## CULTIVATION

Pear trees must have a sheltered, warm site and fertile, free-draining, but moisture-retentive soil. Add plenty of organic material while preparing the ground. Set out new plants at any favourable time between late autumn and spring. Planting distances vary according to the type of plant. Bush trees can be up to 4.5m/15ft apart, dwarf pyramids 1.5m/5ft apart, cordons 75cm/30in apart, and espaliers and fans 4.5m/15ft apart. Stake free-standing trees to prevent wind-rock. Mulch with well-rotted manure in the spring. Thoroughly water during dry spells. If the crop is heavy, thin out young fruit in early to midsummer so that they do not touch.

> **ROOTSTOCKS**
>
> As with apples, the rootstock on which a pear tree grows affects the size and rate of growth of the tree.
> **Quince C:** moderately dwarfing stock (bush, cordon, dwarf pyramid, espalier, fan)
> **Quince A:** semi-vigorous stock (bush, cordon, dwarf pyramid, espalier, fan)
> **Pear:** vigorous stock (standard, half-standard)

BELOW These pears have been grown in a cordon against trellis, a method suitable for small gardens.

BELOW 'Conference' pears have a distinctive elongated shape. These healthy specimens are ripe for picking and enjoying.

RIGHT A pear tree trained in the shape of a cone.

PRUNING A DWARF PYRAMID PEAR After planting, cut back the leader by a third. Cut sideshoots back to 15cm/6in. In the first summer cut back new growth on main sideshoots to five leaves and on secondary shoots to three leaves. Thereafter, cut back new growth on the main stems to five leaves and reduce other new growth to one leaf. In winter thin out any congested spurs.

PRUNING AN ESPALIERED PEAR After planting, cut back to two buds above the bottom wire. In the first summer tie the leader to a vertical cane and the next two shoots to canes at 45 degrees. Cut back all other shoots to two leaves. In autumn lower the two sideshoots and tie to the bottom wire. In winter cut back the leader to two buds above the second wire and repeat the above until the espalier covers all the wires.

### PRUNING AND TRAINING

Most varieties of pears are spur-bearers, producing fruit on spurs that grow on two-year-old or older wood. The leader's new growth can, therefore, be safely cut back in winter by about a third of its length, and laterals can be pruned to three or four buds. Spurs are readily produced and should be thinned once the tree is established. Before starting to prune, remove dead, dying or weak growth and then work with what is left.

### HARVESTING AND STORAGE

Early varieties can be picked just before they ripen, but mid-season and late varieties should be left until they are ripe. Pears can be stored in slatted trays in a cool room.

### PESTS AND DISEASES

Pears are prone to a number of pests, including aphids, codling moth and pear midge. Diseases include fireblight, canker, scab and brown rot. Fireblight will probably mean removal of the entire tree.

# Growing cherries

Although cherries are a really delicious fruit, they are not widely grown in gardens. One reason for this is that until relatively recently these vigorous plants could be grown only as large trees. This was a problem in small gardens as well as making it difficult to prevent birds from stealing the whole crop, since it is virtually impossible to net a large tree. Now that dwarfing rootstocks are available, much smaller trees can be grown, and it is worth finding the space to grow them.

There are two types of cherry: sweet cherries (*Prunus avium*) and sour or acid cherries (*P. cerasus*). Sweet cherries are perfect for eating, while the sour varieties, typified by 'Morello' cherries, are cooked or bottled. Most people prefer sweet cherries, but the sour forms are easier to grow in a small garden because they are less vigorous, especially when they are on Colt dwarfing stock. They are also self-fertile, so one tree is sufficient.

If you do not have room for a big tree, sweet cherries are best trained as fans on a warm wall, where their size can be controlled and they can be easily covered against marauding birds. Sweet cherries generally need two varieties in order for pollination to be effective, except for 'Stella', 'Sunburst' and a few other self-fertile varieties.

## CULTIVATION

Cherries need a warm, sunny position, ideally next to a wall. The soil should be well-drained so that it is not waterlogged, but it must be sufficiently moist to provide the precise conditions that cherries like. Plant full-sized trees 9m/30ft apart. Smaller trees and fan-trained cherries can be 4.5–5.5m/15–18ft apart. Stake young trees firmly so that the lower part of the trunk and the rootball are not rocked by the wind. If possible, mulch with well-rotted manure or other organic material to help retain moisture. Water cherry trees in dry spells but keep the level of moisture even, because a sudden glut of water after a dry spell is likely to cause the fruit to crack, which ruins it. There is no need to thin cherries.

## PRUNING AND TRAINING

Sweet cherry trees need little pruning, apart from the removal of dead or damaged growth, unless they are trained as fans, when new growth is cut back to five leaves

SOUR CHERRY BUSH OR TREE Once established, bush and full-sized sour cherry trees need little pruning other than to remove a third of the old fruiting wood, cutting back to a new growth. Also remove any crossing branches.

SOUR CHERRY FAN Once established, there are two purposes to pruning a cherry fan: to keep the fan shape and to ensure that there is a constant supply of new wood. To keep the shape completely, remove any shoots that are pointing in the wrong direction. For renewal, cut back in summer all shoots that have fruited, preferably as far back as the next new shoot. Tie these new shoots to the cane and wire framework.

every summer. In early spring remove all new side growth. Sour cherries grow on year-old wood, and so some of the older wood is removed each year so that new growth is produced. After picking the fruit in summer, cut back one-year-old shoots on which the fruit was borne to the first new growth. In early summer reduce the number of new sideshoots to about one every 8cm/3in. Remove all shoots that face towards or away from the wall. Remove any "water" shoots that appear from the bottom of the tree. Bush and full-size trees need little pruning.

## HARVESTING AND STORAGE
Pick sweet cherries as they become ripe. If you have a lot of cherries to pick, early in the morning is the best time because the leaves are crisp and stand up, revealing the fruit. Later in the day, especially if it is hot, the leaves tend to be limp and hang over the fruit. Pick the fruit with the stalks on. The stalks of sour cherries should be cut rather than pulled to avoid tearing, which would allow disease to enter. Cherries can be frozen or bottled. They should be stoned (pitted) first.

## PESTS AND DISEASES
Birds are the worst problem; given the chance, they will eat every cherry long before the gardener can get to them. Aphids can also be a problem. Canker, silverleaf – a serious fungal disease affecting plums as well as cherries – and brown rot are the most likely diseases to watch out for.

ABOVE This fan-trained cherry has been netted to protect it against birds. Here, it is trained against wires, but it could also be trained against a wall or fence.

BELOW Ripe cherries ready for harvesting. The fruit should be picked with the stalks in place so that the flesh is not damaged.

# Growing plums and damsons

The word "plum" actually encompasses a great diversity of fruit, including damsons, bullaces and the gages. Plums come in all shapes and sizes, and as with the other main tree fruits, distinctive cultivars have been developed for dessert purposes and for cooking. The former are succulent and mouthwatering; the latter are firmer and less sweet.

In general, plums like a sunny situation, but there are plums for all sorts of climates, and you may well find that some are better suited to local conditions than others. Check to see what varieties are grown in your particular area.

Plums are mainly grown as trees, varying from full-sized standards to spindle bushes and pyramids. They can also be trained as fans. Unfortunately, they cannot be grown as cordons. Plum trees are not usually large and can be accommodated in small gardens.

Damsons can be planted in a hedge, saving a lot of space and yet producing a good crop of fruit. Plums vary in fertility, some being self-fertile, but they all do better for having a pollinator in the area.

## CULTIVATION

Plums must have a sunny position; in cooler areas, a position against a wall will be ideal. They flower early and so should not be planted in frost pockets. The soil should be fertile and moisture retentive, although they will tolerate drier soil than many other tree fruits. Plant the trees at any time between autumn and early spring, as long as weather and soil conditions allow. Planting distance will vary from 3m/10ft to 7.5m/25ft, depending on the size of tree. Fan-trained trees will need to be 3–4.5m/10–15ft apart. Smaller trees and fan-trained varieties should be covered if frost threatens while they are in blossom. Mulch in early spring. If the crop is heavy, thin the fruit as soon as the stones begin to form. Thin so that they are 5–8cm/2–3in apart.

> ### ROOTSTOCKS
> The rootstock on which a plum tree grows affects the size and rate of growth.
> **Pixy:** dwarfing stock (bush, pyramid)
> **St Julien A:** semi-vigorous stock (bush, fan, pyramid)
> **Damas C:** moderately vigorous stock (half-standard)
> **Brompton:** vigorous stock (half-standard, standard)
> **Myrobalan B:** vigorous stock (half-standard, standard)

ABOVE A cluster of plums that would have benefited from thinning out – they are growing too close together.

PRUNING A PLUM FAN IN SPRING AND SUMMER The main aim when pruning a plum fan is to maintain the fan shape. In spring cut out any new sideshoots that are pointing towards or away from the wall. If necessary, reduce the number of new shoots to about one every 15cm/6in. In summer cut back all new shoots to about six leaves, leaving any that are needed to fill in gaps in the main framework. In autumn, after cropping, further cut back the shoots to three leaves.

RIGHT In late summer, wall fruits can be tied in to prevent damage from autumn winds. Pruning members of the plum family should be kept to a minimum to avoid infection from silverleaf disease.

## PRUNING AND TRAINING

Any pruning should be carried out in summer to reduce the chances of the tree being infected with silverleaf, a serious disease of plums and cherries. Once the initial shape has been determined, larger trees do not need any pruning apart from the removal of misplaced, dead or damaged wood. On fans, remove all new shoots that face towards or away from the wall. Shorten any retained new growth to six leaves.

## HARVESTING AND STORAGE

Pick the plums as they ripen. For cooking and preserving pick a little earlier, just before the fruit is ripe. Keep the stalk on the fruit as you pick them. They can be frozen or bottled for storage, but it is best to remove the stones first.

## PESTS AND DISEASES

Wasps and birds can cause problems, as can larger animals such as rabbits and hares. Other insect pests include aphids and winter moths. The main diseases are silverleaf, canker and brown rot. Trees that are badly affected with silverleaf and canker should be burnt or destroyed at once.

RIGHT Ripening damsons are suitable for cooking once they have coloured. Eat them fresh when they are fully ripe.

CULTIVATING TREE FRUIT

# Growing peaches and nectarines

Peaches and nectarines are closely related and they are treated similarly in the garden, although nectarines do better in warmer conditions and are less hardy. Both fruits can be grown as free-standing trees, but in cooler climates both are better grown as fans against a sunny wall or fence.

## CULTIVATION

Peaches and nectarines need a warm, sunny site. The soil should be free draining but moist, so add plenty of organic material. Plant the trees or fans in autumn or early winter, with both at a distance of 4.5m/15ft. Trees should be staked to avoid wind-rock. Mulch in the spring with a good layer of manure or garden compost. A plastic canopy to keep rain off during winter and early spring will protect against peach leaf curl. Protect the blossom from frost, if necessary, with horticultural fleece. Water during dry periods.

PEACH BUSH TREE Not a great deal of pruning is required for a peach bush tree. In spring, cut back some of the older barren wood as far as a replacement new shoot. Also remove any awkwardly placed branches and keep the bush open and airy. Avoid making large cuts, as this is likely to allow canker to infect the tree.

## PRUNING AND TRAINING

Mature trees do not require much pruning apart from the removal of dead or damaged wood and the cutting out of some of the older wood to promote new, vigorous growth. Remove all the shoots that face towards or away from the wall. Initially, thin other shoots to intervals of about 15cm/6in, tying them to the wires and removing the tips if they are longer than about 45cm/18in. Once the plant is established, allow a new bud to form at the base of each lateral in spring, but remove all other buds.

After fruiting, remove the fruiting wood and tie in the new lateral to replace it. Remove the tip if it is too long.

## HARVESTING AND STORAGE

Pick the fruit as it ripens. It is best eaten straight from the tree but can be kept for a few days in a cool place. It can be stored for longer periods by freezing or bottling.

## PESTS AND DISEASES

Birds and aphids are common problems with peaches and nectarines, as are earwigs and red spider mite. Diseases include peach leaf curl, powdery mildew and canker.

> **ROOTSTOCKS**
>
> The rootstock will affect the size and rate of growth of the tree.
> **St Julien A:** semi-vigorous stock (bush, fan)
> **Brompton:** vigorous stock (bush)

LEFT Fan-trained peaches, such as this healthy specimen, provide a decorative feature for a wall.

# Growing apricots

Apricots are not grown as often as most other fruit, partly because they are not very easy to grow and partly because, with limited space, most gardeners prefer to grow the more luscious peaches. However, home-grown apricots taste much better than shop-bought fruit.

One of the problems with apricots is that they flower very early and are susceptible to frosts. They are, therefore, suitable only for warm areas. Their need for warmth means that they are best grown as fans against a sunny wall, which will help to protect them from the cold. They are self-fertile, so there is no need for different varieties.

## CULTIVATION

A warm, sunny, frost-free site is required to grow apricots successfully. The soil should be free draining but moisture retentive. Apricots do best in soil that is slightly alkaline. You will have to incorporate plenty of organic material before planting. Plant in autumn or early winter, placing fans about 4.5m/15ft apart. The blossom needs to be protected if there is a possibility of frost. Mulch the ground with manure and keep the ground watered during dry spells. If there is a potentially heavy crop, thin out the fruits to about 8cm/3in apart.

## PRUNING AND TRAINING

On mature fans, thin new laterals in early summer to 15cm/6in apart, shortening those remaining to 5–6 leaves (unless they are needed to fill gaps in the framework). Shorten them to three leaves after fruiting. Apart from that, little pruning is required because most apricot fruit is borne on old wood. Every few years, remove some of the older wood and allow new laterals to develop in order to replace it.

> **ROOTSTOCKS**
> The rootstock will affect the size and rate of growth of the tree.
> **St Julien A**: semi-vigorous stock (bush, fan)
> **Brompton**: vigorous stock (bush)

## HARVESTING AND STORAGE

Pick the fruit once it has fully ripened and can be removed easily from the stalk. Apricots do not store well, although they can be frozen or dried.

## PESTS AND DISEASES

Protect fruit from birds by netting. Aphids may also be a problem. The most likely diseases are silverleaf, canker, brown rot, grey mould (botrytis) and dieback.

BELOW An elegant fan-trained apricot tree spread out across a large wall. The canes, supported by wires, help to maintain the fan shape.

APRICOT FAN Once the fan has been established, the object of most pruning is to maintain the shape. In early summer, cut out any shoots that are pointing in the wrong direction, especially those that point towards or away from the wall. Thin new shoots, leaving one every 15cm/6in. Prune the remaining shoots to five leaves and again, after fruiting, back to three leaves.

# Growing citrus fruits

In Mediterranean climates citrus trees can be grown outside all year round, and in more temperate climates they can be successfully grown in containers, keeping them under glass over winter and putting them out to enjoy the summer sun. In fact, you can grow some citrus fruits without a conservatory to house them; mandarins, for example, fruit well at a small size indoors. More problems will be caused by poor ventilation than by low temperatures.

BELOW Given the conditions they enjoy, citrus fruits will grow continually even in fairly small pots, producing fruit from an early age.

RIGHT Citrus fruits, perfect for conservatory production in cold climates, make charming feature plants for warmer gardens, having fragrant blossom, fine evergreen foliage and edible fruits.

## CULTIVATION

Contrary to popular opinion, citrus plants are not difficult to grow, provided you do not pamper them into poor health. First, don't keep them in high temperatures all year round; they are fine in frost-free glasshouses in winter and can even stand a touch of frost. Satsumas and kumquats are especially hardy, to -10°C/14°F. The important point is to adjust them to different temperatures, moving them

outdoors gradually. They will be happier outdoors than sweltering in a hot, humid conservatory, so bring them out as early as possible; they will be more susceptible to pests if they are kept indoors.

ABOVE Citrus trees prefer cool rather than hot conditions. If they are grown in cold climates, they should be kept outside in summer and in a frost-free conservatory or greenhouse throughout the winter months.

ABOVE Lemons become paler and lose some juiciness and acidity after they ripen, so always pick deep yellow specimens. The fruits do not continue to develop after picking, giving them excellent keeping qualities.

Second, many people overwater citrus plants, which causes the fruit and leaves to drop. The best approach is to water plants only when the compost (planting mix) is dry to a depth of 5cm/2in, and then water thoroughly so that it flushes right through the compost. That way, if your tap water is very hard, excess lime is flushed away too. At most, water once weekly in summer, and every three weeks in winter.

Because citrus fruits are high-performance evergreens, they need a constant if low-level supply of nutrients, so use a specialist feed with every watering and apply it also as a regenerative spray-on foliar feed. Citrus will do best in soilless, fairly acid compost because it dries out more quickly than soil-based mixes.

## PRUNING

There is no art to citrus pruning. Because the plants are continuously growing, they can become quite leggy, so cut them hard back. As long as you cut above the graft union – look low down on the trunk or stem – you will not harm the plant. Better still is to keep pinching them out regularly during spring and summer.

## HARVESTING AND STORAGE

Once the fruits have ripened to their yellow, orange or green colours, they can be picked and stored for several weeks.

RIGHT The newly ripening green fruit and fragrant white flowers of the lemon tree often appear at the same time, making them particularly attractive conservatory plants.

## PESTS AND DISEASES

Red spider mite, scale insects, mealy bugs, aphids and whitefly may be problems for citrus trees. Keep them under control by wiping the leaves with a little dishwashing detergent and water.

# Index

acid and alkaline soils 27
animals 44, 59
apples 6, 7, 9, 10–11, 33, 38, 42, 43, 52–3, 54
apricots 7, 9, 20, 33, 39, 41, 42–3, 61

biological controls 47
birds 40, 44, 47, 53, 56, 57, 59, 60, 61
bottling 43, 57, 59, 60
bullaces 58
buying fruit trees 32

cherries 7, 14–15, 32, 39, 42, 56–7
choosing fruit trees 32–3
citrus fruits 9, 21–3, 43, 62–3
clay soils 26
compost 28, 29, 30–1, 46
containers 9, 33, 34, 51, 62
cooking 7, 11, 17, 20
  preparation 13, 15, 19, 21, 23
cordons 6, 25, 33, 36, 38, 39, 41, 52, 54, 58

damsons 7, 16–17, 38–9, 42, 43, 58–9
digging 28, 34

diseases 32, 38, 39, 41, 45, 46, 53, 55, 57, 59, 60, 61, 63
drying 43, 61

equipment 48–9
espaliers 6, 25, 33, 36, 38, 41, 54

fans 33, 36, 39, 41, 54, 56, 58, 60
fleece 41, 52, 60
freezing 7, 43, 53, 57, 59, 60, 61
fruit cages 40

grapefruits 21
greengages 7, 33, 38–9, 58
grit 27, 34

harvesting 7, 42–3, 53, 55, 57, 59, 60, 61, 63

insects 44–5, 47, 53, 55, 56, 57, 59, 60, 61, 63

kumquats 22

labelling 35, 49
ladders 38
leafmould 29
lemons 7, 21
limes 22
loam 26–7

mulching 35, 46, 52, 54, 56, 58, 60, 61

nectarines 7, 9, 18–19, 33, 39, 41, 42, 60
nutrition 6, 11, 13, 15, 17, 19, 20, 21

oranges 7, 22–3
organic cultivation 6, 27, 28, 34, 46–7, 52, 54, 56, 60, 61

peaches 6, 7, 9, 18–19, 33, 39, 41, 42, 60
pears 7, 9, 12–13, 33, 38, 42, 43, 54–5
peat 46
pests 44–5, 46, 53, 55, 57, 59, 60, 61, 63
planting 34–5, 52, 54, 56, 58, 60, 61
plums 6, 7, 16–17, 32, 33, 38–9, 42, 43, 58–9
predators 47
preserving 43
protecting fruit 9, 40–1, 52, 58, 60, 61
pruning 6, 38–9, 52–3, 55, 56–7, 59, 60, 61, 63

rootstocks 32, 52, 54, 58, 60, 61
  dwarf 6, 33, 51, 56

sandy soils 26
secateurs (pruners) 38, 42, 43, 48
soil 48
  improving 27, 28–9, 46
  preparation 25, 34
  types 26–7
storing 7, 11, 13, 15, 17, 19, 20, 23, 42–3, 53, 55, 57, 59, 60, 61, 63
supporting fruit trees 25, 35, 36–7, 52–3, 54, 56, 60

tangerines 22
thinning 53, 54, 56, 58, 61
tools 48–9
top-dressing 28–9

watering 54, 56, 60, 61, 63
weeding 34, 35

The publisher would like to thank *The Garden Picture Library* for supplying the picture on p57t.